Awaken Your
Strongest Self

Break Free of Stress,

Inner Conflict, and Self-Sabotage

NEIL FIORE, Ph.D.

New York Chicago San Francisco Lisbon London Madrid Mexico City
Milan New Delhi San Juan Seoul Singapore Sydney Toronto

Library of Congress Cataloging-in-Publication Data

Fiore, Neil A.
    Awaken your strongest self : break free of stress, inner conflict, and self-sabotage / by Neil A. Fiore.
        p.   cm.
    Includes bibliographical references and index.
    ISBN 0-07-147026-3
    1. Negativism.   2. Self-actualization (Psychology).   3. Leadership.
4. Self-help techniques.   I. Title.

BF698.35. N44F56   2007
158.1—dc22   2006009598

This book is dedicated to my parents,
Esther and Anthony Fiore, who gave me
a sense of innate worth and the loving acceptance
to develop my own Strongest Self. And also to my therapy and
coaching clients, who have helped me refine this process
over the last twenty years.

3 4 5 6 7 8 9 10 11 12 13 14 15 16 17 18 19 20 21 22   DOC/DOC   0 9 8

ISBN 978-0-07-147026-1
MHID   0-07-147026-3

Interior design by Monica Baziuk

McGraw-Hill books are available at special quantity discounts to use as premiums and sales promotions or for use in corporate training programs. To contact a representative, please visit the Contact Us pages at www.mhprofessional.com.

This book is printed on acid-free paper.

Contents

Acknowledgments

I COULD NOT HAVE WRITTEN this book without the encouragement of my therapy and coaching clients, who motivated me to put the Awaken Your Strongest Self process down in writing. I am enormously grateful to clients and friends who were willing to have the stories of their longing for a more joyful and fulfilling life shared with the readers of this book.

I especially want to thank Lauren Cox-Pursley, Melanie Rigney, and my niece Debra Sutton for their editorial help, guidance, and recommendations; Barbara Van Diest for her wise coaching; my sister Nancy Hershbain for her support and encouragement; and the many readers of early drafts, especially Pam Rudd and Jane Sterzlinger. I am indebted to Dr. Chris Duis for her consultations on neuropsychology and to Drs. Sonia Lippke and Ralf Schwarzer of the Free University of Berlin for their excellent research on the stages of health behavior change and for their personal support. My agents, Sheree Bykofsky and Janet Rosen, deserve a special acknowledgment for their sage advice and instantaneous responses, as does Natasha Graf, my editor at McGraw-Hill, whose generous enthusiasm for this book has kept me inspired throughout.

The development of the concepts, processes, and exercises in this book has been influenced directly and indirectly by my larger support system of innumerable teachers, writers, and researchers,

as well as from feedback from my clients and workshop partici-
pants. Among the primary resources that deserve acknowledg-
ment are Roberto Assagioli, Sylvia Boorstein, Joan Borysenko,
Joseph Campbell, Mihaly Csikszentmihalyi, the Dalai Lama, Ram
Dass, Teilhard de Chardin, Anthony de Mello, Wayne Dyer, Mil-
ton H. Erickson, Matthew Fox, Erich Fromm, Tim Gallwey,
Thich Nhat Hanh, Kabir Edmund Helminski, Jean Houston, Carl
Jung, Louise Kaplan, Jack Kornfield, Harold Kushner, George
Leonard, Stephen Levine, Donald Meichenbaum, Dan Millman,
Wayne Muller, Michael Murphy, Robert Ornstein, Wendy
Palmer, James Pennebaker, Fritz Perls, H. W. L. Poonja, David
Richo, John C. Robinson, Ernest Rossi, Martin Seligman, Her-
bert and David Spiegel, Charles Spielberger, Richard Suinn, D. T.
Suzuki, Shunryu Suzuki, Leslie Temple-Thurston, John and
Helen Watkins, Alan Watts, John Welwood, Ken Wilber, and
Colin Wilson.

An Important Note: The identities of all patients and clients
described in the examples presented in this book have been
altered to protect their confidentiality.

Introduction

The Sleeper Must Awaken

A person needs new experiences. . . . Without change something sleeps inside us and seldom awakens. The sleeper must awaken.
—Duke Leto in Frank Herbert's *Dune*

THIRTY YEARS AGO I underwent nine months of weekly chemotherapy to treat cancer that the doctor told me had spread to my lung. That experience awakened in me a new appreciation for life that didn't leave time or energy for worrying about the small stuff of life. If you, like me, have ever narrowly escaped a tragedy and had a wake-up call, you probably discovered, as I did, a profound gratitude for just being alive and a deep appreciation for your loved ones. But have you ever wondered who the wake-up call is for and who's been asleep? I believe that it's for your Strongest Self —the *you* who's been waiting to unlock the full potential of your new, human brain.

This book's four-step program will show you how to awaken your Strongest Self *without* needing a dangerous wake-up call. You'll learn how to use the uniquely human part of your new brain—which neuroscientists label the executive organizing functions of the prefrontal cortex, located in the center of the forehead—to live more fully, joyfully, and effectively.

Over the last two million years, the hominid skull has expanded to accommodate the monitoring, planning, socializing, and leadership functions of our modern prefrontal cortex. The skulls of apes, chimpanzees, *Homo erectus*, and Neanderthals have pronounced eyebrow ridges and backward slanted foreheads, revealing an underdeveloped frontal lobe that lacked the executive regulatory functions and self-reflective consciousness that make you human. The expanded prefrontal cortex of modern humans (*Homo sapiens sapiens*), however, has moved our foreheads to a near-vertical position and increased the average size of our brain to 1,350 cubic centimeters. Much of this development has taken place in the last 120,000 years.

This relatively new, and most recently evolved, part of the human brain monitors, coordinates, and regulates the activities of a 500-million-year-old reptile brain, a 200-million-year-old mammal brain, and a 50-million-year-old primate brain. All of these separate and distinct brain regions and functions coexist, more or less peacefully, inside your skull. "The human brain is a compendium of circuits piled atop one another . . . so we do not have one single brain but a multilevel brain, built in different eras for different priorities," writes Dr. Robert Ornstein in *Multimind*. It's the interaction and integration of these systems and functions that make you a coherent person with integrity rather than a series of separate, unpredictable reactions. Someone must direct these multiple brains and update default responses that were set millions of years ago to survive in environments and cultures very different from those of today. That someone is your Strongest Self, which acts like a separate mind with the job of determining your higher values, adapting to changing environments, and integrating lower brain functions into a coherent whole.

The Benefits of Connecting to Your Strongest Self

Every week, I work with twenty or more therapy and coaching clients who are talented and motivated people just like you. And it pains me to see them struggling so hard against blocks to happiness, effectiveness, and inner peace. I've written this book so you can benefit from the practices that have helped thousands break free of counterproductive patterns, discover their true potential, and warm to life the parts of them that have been frozen away and dormant.

You'll see that this book doesn't insist that you try harder using the same old, ineffective tools that come from a limited sense of self and the automatic reactions of primitive brains. Indeed, the parts of you that have been fearful, resistant, and unsure will no longer be in charge of your life. You'll be acting from your human brain—the newest and most powerful brain on the planet!

The exciting news is that *Awaken Your Strongest Self* gives you the tools to unlock your full potential as the leader and effective manager of your life. It helps you shift out of a limited perspective of your abilities and into the roles that will empower you to live a life of greater joy, ease, and effectiveness without having to wait for your lower brain functions to feel confident and motivated.

Wake Up Your "New Brain"

Over the last fifty million years of primate evolution, the size of the prefrontal cortex has expanded to more than 30 percent of the neocortex in humans, compared with 11.5 percent in monkeys and 17 percent in chimpanzees. The expanded prefrontal cortex of humans includes a working memory, planning and anticipation, the ability to choose, neuronal adaptability (or plasticity), and the ability to form associations and representations that give us unique cognitive skills for language, creativity, inventiveness, and goal achievement.

Recent studies by neuroscientists using functional magnetic resonance imaging (fMRI) scans show that the *new brain* (the prefrontal cortex) lights up when those in deep meditation and prayer attain feelings of transcendence, inner peace, and improved concentration. They also experience a greater sense of connection within themselves and with the world.

By using the Awaken Your Strongest Self four-step program, you'll be lighting up—and waking up—your human brain's organizing and regulating capabilities to play their proper leadership role in managing and guiding your life. When you apply this program to your life, you'll learn to recognize the automatic and conditioned reactions of your more primitive brains. From that recognition, you'll be able to use your distinctly human ability to *choose to act* in ways congruent with your higher purpose, vision, and evolved values.

Break Free of Self-Destructive Patterns and Fear

The Awaken Your Strongest Self program gives you the skills you need to connect to what British psychiatrist Anthony Storr calls "something superior to the ego." This something is often referred to as the self, subconscious mind, universe, a higher power, the genius, inner strength, soul, or spirit.

In keeping with this book's nonsectarian approach, I refer to this something as the Strongest Self and its key roles as the protective self and leadership self. Your ego (which includes your personality, conscious mind, and everyday identity, not the psychoanalytic or Freudian use of the term *ego*) is only a part of your Strongest Self. With practice you'll learn to connect your ego to the larger support system of your Strongest Self and to train your ego to surrender its lonely, arrogant struggle.

This program shows you how to play a leadership role in your life. It shows you how to free yourself from the obsolete patterns and fears that are keeping you from experiencing your full potential and achieving your higher goals. Note that acknowledging the evolution of the human brain and the advent of consciousness on the planet doesn't exclude belief in God, a higher power, or a higher wisdom in the universe. In fact, it's congruent with the concept of exercising our uniquely human ability of free will to choose actions that distinguish us from the animals and our lower brains. You can make this program work for you without having to change your religious or spiritual beliefs.

Achieve Your Goals with Less Struggle and Greater Peace

By applying the exercises and tools in this book, most of my clients have attained a greater sense of inner peace while achieving their most important goals. Following these methods, one of my clients, the owner of a small business, doubled her income while working fewer hours. Another client, a man who weighed 380 pounds, lost 110 pounds in one year without ever feeling as if he were on a diet. Another stopped smoking before his daughter's wedding, while still another used these methods to pass the state bar exam on her eighth try. One man overcame a lifetime of aggressive type A behavior and became, in his words, "like a Buddha in rush-hour traffic." Another conquered procrastination and completed and mailed off five years of back taxes. And as you'll read in later chapters, I was able to cope with a devastating cancer diagnosis and a difficult treatment process.

More important than the goals my clients and I achieved is *how easily* we achieved them—once we learned to go beyond struggling from our conscious mind/ego to connect with something superior. By letting go of a limited sense of identity and connecting with their Strongest Self, my clients have been able to complete books, screenplays, and doctoral dissertations and to overcome their fear and produce their first musical CDs. One even overcame her stage fright and sang in the Paris Opera! Younger clients have learned to cope with attention deficit disorder (ADD) to graduate high school and enter college.

Ordinary people including myself have found that facing a wide variety of challenges from the perspective of our Strongest Selves and new brain (as I instruct in this book) has freed us from outdated, destructive patterns of behavior. The concepts and exercises in this book will set you rapidly on your way to aligning your actions with your higher values and goals.

Following the Four Steps to Achieve Your Full Potential

What steps did we follow to achieve our goals and fulfill our dreams? In essence, we followed the four steps outlined in this book. And you can, too.

In "Step 1: Step Back from Your Old, Ineffective Patterns," you'll learn to recognize the specific words, feelings, and physical sensations that make up your instinctual and learned ego reactions to life's pressures. With the help of the fear inoculation exercises in Chapter 1, you'll develop your ability to recognize your automatic, reactive habits before they can pull you into hours and days of emotional upset. You'll learn how to break through fear and self-doubt and start the process of replacing outdated patterns with healthier alternatives.

In "Step 2: Step Up to Your New Brain and Your Strongest Self," you'll learn how to shift to a new perspective that awakens your leadership strengths. You'll find that playing a protective role and gaining a leader's perspective free you from your former fears, struggles, and feelings of being overwhelmed. Applying a new point of view from the vantage point of your new brain, you'll break away from your personal and prehistoric past. You'll be empowered to direct your attention toward your current challenges, opportunities, and goals.

In "Step 3: Awaken the Five Qualities of Your Strongest Self," you'll discover the five qualities of safety, choice, presence, focus, and connection. With these qualities you'll live more fully by accessing resources that far exceed those of your ego and conscious mind. Learning to make these five qualities a part of your daily commitment to yourself will enable you to quickly shift from fear-based patterns to a stronger, more expansive sense of self. When you start living from your Strongest Self, you'll be able to minimize these five major problem areas—stress, inner conflict, self-criticism, feeling overwhelmed, and struggle—while maximizing joy, focus, inner strength, and your ability to deepen your personal relationships.

In "Step 4: Awaken the Leader in You to Achieve Your Goals," you'll use self-leadership skills to acknowledge the concerns of all aspects of yourself. You'll also forge all levels of your brain into a team congruent with your current mission and focused on achieving your higher goals. You'll find that self-sabotage, procrastination, and ambivalence are virtually eliminated when you take charge of your inner team. Achieving goals happens rapidly, and almost effortlessly, when you awaken to your leadership role and align all parts with your higher vision and values. You'll learn to apply the latest research on the stages of effective change to ensure that you not only begin a process of change but also have the skills and mental toughness to maintain your healthy habits.

When you use this four-step program daily, you'll gain the confidence that—in spite of self-doubts and past failures—you can act more effectively and consistently in accord with your higher values and mission.

Pretest to Measure Your Progress

To start, use these measures to record your current state so you can see your progress over the next few weeks. In the next chapter you'll identify the obstacles you want to eliminate by putting into action the four steps to awaken your Strongest Self.

To measure your progress over the course of this dynamic program, you can record your current levels of stress, joy, inner peace, and feelings of connection to deeper resources on the scales that follow. In Appendix F you'll find a posttest that you can use as a comparison with your current levels to show you how much you've progressed in lowering stress and attaining a greater sense of inner peace by awakening your Strongest Self. Imagine that these scales are thermometers to record your current levels of stress, joy, inner peace, and connection.

1. Stress

Circle the number that indicates your average level of stress for the past week.

NONE									THE MOST EVER	
0	10	20	30	40	50	60	70	(80)	90	100

2. Joy

Circle the number that indicates your average level of joy for the past week.

NONE									THE MOST EVER	
0	10	20	(30)	40	50	60	70	80	90	100

3. Inner Peace

Circle the number that indicates your average level of inner peace for the past week.

NONE									THE MOST EVER	
0	10	20	(30)	40	50	60	70	80	90	100

4. Connection

Circle the number that indicates your average level of feeling connected to something stronger than yourself for the past week.

NONE									THE MOST EVER	
0	(10)	20	30	40	50	60	70	80	90	100

Pretest to Measure Your Intention and Commitment

The latest research on personal effectiveness, or self-efficacy, and the maintenance of long-term health habits—such as regular exercise, diet improvement, and smoking cessation—shows that perceived control and behavioral intention are among the key qualities that predict success. By learning to shift to your new brain's organizing functions—especially choice, regulation of anxiety and arousal, long-term commitment, and overriding lower brain reactivity—you'll become more certain that when you set a goal from your higher, Strongest Self it will have the cooperation of every part of you. When you truly intend and commit to an action, it will have behind it the full power of your Strongest Self's leadership perspective and deep resources.

The following five scales will give you a subjective measure of your current estimates of your desire, ability, confidence, control, and intention to improve, change, and take charge of your life.

1. Desire/Motivation

How much do you want to improve, change, and take charge of your life?

DEFINITELY DO NOT   DEFINITELY DO

| 1 | 2 | 3 | 4 | 5 | (6) | 7 | 8 | 9 | 10 |

2. Ability

To what extent do you see yourself as being capable of making improvements, creating positive change, and taking charge of your life?

INCAPABLE   CAPABLE

| 1 | 2 | 3 | 4 | 5 | 6 | 7 | (8) | 9 | 10 |

3. Confidence

How confident are you that you will improve, change, and take charge of your life?

NOT VERY CONFIDENT   VERY CONFIDENT

| 1 | 2 | 3 | 4 | (5) | 6 | 7 | 8 | 9 | 10 |

4. Perceived Control

How much personal control do you feel you have over making improvements, changing habits, and taking charge of your life?

NO CONTROL   COMPLETE CONTROL

| 1 | 2 | 3 | 4 | 5 | 6 | (7) | 8 | 9 | 10 |

5. Intention

How often do you intend to use the exercises and concepts in this book to make improvements, change habits, and take charge of your life?

NEVER   FREQUENTLY

| 1 | 2 | 3 | 4 | 5 | 6 | 7 | 8 | 9 | 10 |

Read this book slowly, perhaps a chapter at a time, and apply its concepts, strategies, and tools in your life. You'll be learning new concepts—or, at the very least, new ways to apply these concepts—so refer back to the book to remind yourself of its motivating stories and exercises. You may want to keep a notebook and pen handy while reading this book to record your experiences with each exercise and the negative patterns you'll be indentifying.

Expect a dynamic inner shift in attitude, perspective, and ability. The exercises in each chapter will help you integrate new skills into your life that will connect you to your inner resources and strengths. To attain these goals, you'll need to experiment with and use these concepts and exercises in your life every day. Within weeks, you'll unlock the leadership power of your new brain and you'll find that the smaller, fearful parts of you will follow your lead. Finally, *you*—as your Strongest Self—will be in charge of your life.

Step Back from Your Old, Ineffective Patterns

1

Five Signs That You Are Not Your Strongest Self . . . Yet

All the greatest and most important problems of life are fundamentally unsolvable; they only fade when confronted with a new and stronger life passion.

— Carl G. Jung

DURING MY TWENTY-FIVE YEARS as a psychologist and ten years as a life coach, I've discovered that if you want to reach your true potential, it's much more effective to ignite a new passion for life than to dwell on past problems. We begin our process, however, by identifying five major problem areas and reactive patterns so you can quickly replace them with the action steps, leadership, and qualities of your Strongest Self. Learning to recognize your old patterns as small parts of a much larger self is the first essential step toward transformative change.

The practice of observing your thoughts, feelings, and impulses awakens your higher brain to be conscious of lower brain automatic reactions and to exercise its executive ability to choose how to act. By observing your thoughts, behavior, and moods, you gain some needed distance and time to choose actions that are congruent with your values and consistent with who you wish to become. This process also changes the structure of your brain, making it more flexible and adaptable as you add more neural connections between your executive organizing functions and your ancestral brains.

The practice of meditation works in a similar way. You notice your thoughts and impulses as they arise, and you become aware that a part of you is always calmly observing. As you shift your sense of self into the perspective of that observer, you are less likely to be pulled into distracting thoughts or reactive impulses. Distractions such as the familiar bells of the ice-cream truck outside your door automatically trigger your desire for ice cream, but you don't have to follow your lower brain's urge to jump up, chase after the vendor, and buy some ice cream. Instead, you can observe your thoughts and cravings, focus on your breathing, and *choose* to sit still. You can watch your thoughts and feelings change and fade away.

Whenever you exercise your freedom of choice, you are doing more than just passively observing. You are awakening and activating your uniquely human ability to override your initial, lower brain reactions in order to choose how to act.

Choosing to Face Your Fears

The ability to disidentify from your initial thoughts and reactions is what makes you truly human, and it only exists in your new, human brain—the prefrontal cortex whose rapid expansion has pushed the forehead into a vertical position.

As you awaken more of your uniquely human skills, you'll be able to *choose* to face fear rather than be controlled by it. Each time you choose to face a fear, you're preventing your mammal brain from controlling your behavior and your life. All mammals have a fear of fire, but about two million years ago our early ancestor *Homo erectus* learned to overcome that mammal instinct in order to harness fire for warmth and cooking. By facing a fear you've been avoiding, you break free of lower brain phobias and win a *fear inoculation shot* that makes you more robust against future fears and challenges. Your fear inoculation shots will break the cycle of inertia, avoidance, and guilt while increasing your momentum and motivation.

Identifying Your Five Major Problem Areas

An understanding of the architecture of the human brain is useful in coping with many of life's challenges and the five major problem areas. You can see in Figure 1.1 that the reptile brain (brain stem) is shaped like a carrot that grows up from the top of the spinal column. The old mammal brain (limbic system)—found in ancient rodents and modern cats and dogs—surrounds the reptile brain and adds to it the ability to learn and to relate within a community.

As you can see in Figure 1.2, most of the human brain is made of what looks like a piece of coral, which is about the size of a

FIGURE 1.1 Reptile and Mammal Brains

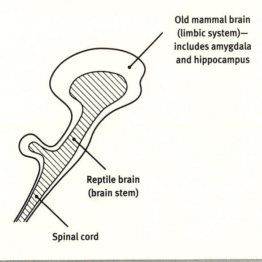

Old mammal brain
(limbic system)—
includes amygdala
and hippocampus

Reptile brain
(brain stem)

Spinal cord

melon, that surrounds and lies atop the mammal and reptile brains. This expansion beyond the earlier brains is called the neocortex, or primate brain. Because our human brain is built upon —and retains many of the features of—the brains of our ancestors, the task of managing our thoughts and actions would be nearly impossible if it were not for our prefrontal cortex.

This uniquely human part of our brain, located in the front third of the neocortex, contains our essential executive organizing functions. It is this part of our brain that gives us the capacity for language, organization, planning, self-regulation, and decision making. And it was the rapid growth of the prefrontal cortex over the last two hundred thousand years that has pushed our forehead to a near-vertical position, distinguishing it from the receding forehead of apes and Neanderthals.

FIGURE 1.2 The Human Brain

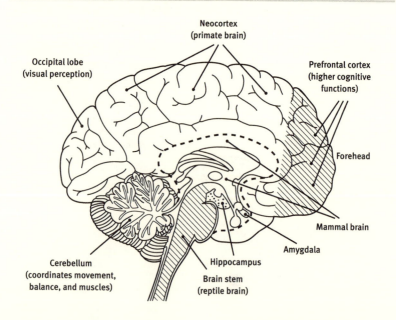

The five major problem areas that can be reduced or resolved by applying the Strongest Self program are:

1. stress and fear
2. inner conflict and procrastination
3. feeling overwhelmed and confused
4. self-criticism and self-blame
5. struggle and loneliness

Within just a few chapters, you'll be shifting your identity away from your symptoms and default reactions and into the perspective, roles, and voice of your Strongest Self. You'll learn to identify the specific words, worries, and physical tensions that signal the use of limited and, usually, primitive methods of coping with current life pressures and challenges. You'll minimize or remove completely the blocks that have kept you from realizing your true potential for happiness, success, and inner peace.

To begin step 1, use the following five problem areas to identify the symptoms that describe your current behavior and negative internal dialogue. Identify and check off your symptoms without self-criticism but with an appreciation that you've taken the first step to freeing yourself of old, destructive patterns.

As you proceed through this program, you'll find it easier to detach from your initial reactions and take control of them if you locate their approximate point of origin in your brain. A fear, fight-or-flight response, for example, originates in the oldest part of the brain—the reptile brain—that has existed for more than five hundred million years. You don't want to argue with a survival response that has obviously worked, but you do want to use your new, executive brain to decide when the danger has passed and when what appears to be a dangerous snake is actually a stick. While snakes were a big problem hundreds of millions of years ago, you might want to reset your old brain's default reaction so that it's more sensitive to the dangers of cars, gangs, and electricity.

Problem Area 1: Stress and Fear

Think about the feelings that arise when you are under time pressure on your job, concerned about bills and spending in your family, worried about your health or medical procedures, or criticized by your partner or family.

Examples of Symptoms
- I frequently feel panicky and anxious, afraid that something awful will happen.
- My ego and self-worth are always on the line (available to be judged by others) at work, in leisure activities, and in my relationships.
- I try to cope with anxiety by relying on a variety of addictive habits or crutches, such as overindulging in coffee, sweets, and alcohol, and becoming dependent in my relationships.
- I attempt to control others and events in the hope of avoiding disappointment and threats to my self-worth.
- I often find it difficult to sleep because my mind races with worries and anxiety.

Negative self-talk: If there's a potential danger, do you say:

- What if something goes wrong? What if they don't like it?
- I couldn't stand it if I fail. If I suffer another loss, I'll feel miserable and worthless.
- I lack confidence and am afraid of what others think about my appearance, my work, and me.

Possible Brain Regions Involved
- Reptile brain fight-or-flight response
- Mammal brain fear of being attacked, abandoned, and shamed by the pack, herd, or family for breaking taboos and rules

- Amygdala emotional response of like and dislike and recognition of fearful and angry faces
- Frontal lobe anticipation of future pain and criticism

You may be lacking the Strongest Self's qualities of safety and self-worth.

Problem Area 2: Inner Conflict and Procrastination

Think of a situation in which you've had difficulty coming to a decision or starting or finishing an important project, and notice which of these symptoms—inner conflict or procrastination— apply.

Examples of Symptoms
- I work hard, but my fear of making a mistake and being criticized causes me to procrastinate and be indecisive.
- I use threats and self-criticism to try to motivate myself, but that only makes things worse.
- I tell myself that I have to do it, but then I feel like I just don't want to do it, which causes inner conflict that stalls my progress and sabotages the achievement of my goals.
- I delay calling my family and friends or clients and customers because I feel guilty and ashamed about not following through on my earlier commitments to them.
- I resent anyone in authority—a parent, teacher, or boss—and resist doing any work I don't want to do.

Negative self-talk: When you typically try to motivate yourself, do you say:

- I should, but I don't want to.
- I have to finish a very important project, must do it perfectly, and must endure a life with no fun.

- I don't want to have to do this.
- I have no choice. I work best under pressure. I just want to get this over with.

Possible Brain Regions Involved
- Mammal brain avoidance of areas associated with past pain
- Mammal brain hormonal reactions that trigger submission, surrender, and yielding as a survival mechanism against attack
- Right brain versus left brain inner conflict between personal wants and the need to learn the rules of the family and society

You may be lacking the Strongest Self's quality of choice.

Problem Area 3: Feeling Overwhelmed and Confused

Think of those situations in which you were juggling several tasks or a large project that would take several weeks or months to complete.

Examples of Symptoms
- I try to do it all and don't know when to ask for help or to acknowledge that the workload and personal responsibilities are too much for me.
- I spend an inordinate amount of time trying to maximize my possibilities and then try to control people and events in a desperate attempt to succeed.
- I have a smorgasbord approach to life, buying every new gadget and fad, with a tendency to gobble lots of objects, food, and people rather than savoring a few.
- I find it difficult to stay focused on one project and am often late or rushing because there are so many things I feel I must accomplish in order to feel good about myself.
- I repeatedly overschedule my day and feel trapped with too many tasks and obligations.

Negative self-talk: When you feel overwhelmed, do you say:

- I want to do it all, but there's too much to do. I don't know where to start.
- I'm running as fast as I can, but I just can't keep up with this workload, and I'm exhausted.
- I'm way behind; I have to catch up.
- What will they do if I can't do it all?

Possible Brain Regions Involved

- Frontal lobe anticipation of future work, challenges, and criticism—as well as hippocampus/amygdala memory of past failures and trauma—that evokes excess energy to try to cope in the two virtual realities of the past and future
- Mammal brain (limbic system) messages of overwhelming and conflicting emotions

You may be lacking the Strongest Self's quality of being centered in the present moment.

Problem Area 4: Self-Criticism and Self-Blame

Think of situations in which you're apt to be self-critical. Especially recall those situations in which you had a lot at stake and wanted to do your best.

Examples of Symptoms

- I believe that a part of me is lazy and needs criticism, threats, and constant nagging in order to perform.
- I feel that whatever I do, it's never good enough, and I should've started the task earlier.
- I seldom accept myself, and if I do it's only when my performance is exceptional.
- I believe that some part of me makes things difficult and sabotages my success.

- I focus on what's wrong with me ("Why did I spill the milk?") rather than on what it takes to just do the job ("How can we clean it up? When do we start?").

Negative self-talk: When you're faced with a challenge or block, do you say:

- There must be something wrong with me. Why do I always spill the milk?
- Why can't I do this? I should be stronger and try harder. I'll never succeed at this rate.
- How will I explain another failure? I've screwed up again.

Possible Brain Regions Involved
- Mammal brain hormonal reactions of submission, surrender, and yielding—as a survival mechanism against attack—that are experienced as shame, low self-esteem, failure, depression, and decreased motivation (an unwillingness to try)
- Left brain internalizing of the rules, critical voice, and fears of parents and teachers

You may be lacking the Strongest Self's qualities of acceptance and task-oriented focus.

Problem Area 5: Struggle and Loneliness
Think of when you kept trying to solve a problem, achieve a goal, or overcome writer's block but couldn't make any progress by just working longer and harder.

Examples of Symptoms
- I'm desperately searching and striving for peace, joy, and fulfillment in something or someone, but I can't seem to find it.
- I feel exhausted and burned out and then try to escape by watching TV, overeating, surfing the Internet, or talking on the phone.

- I work long hours, seldom relax, and then binge on junk food, alcohol, cigarettes, and distractions—but I seldom feel renewed or satisfied.
- I remind myself to be tough (I don't need anybody), but at times I long to surrender to someone or something more powerful than myself.
- I feel I must do everything on my own; there's no one else to support me, no one I can trust to do it as well as me.

Negative self-talk: When you're trying harder and harder, struggling alone to face a challenge, do you say:

- I have to try harder, but I'm tired of working so hard and getting nowhere.
- I've sacrificed and suffered, so I deserve to reward myself with a snack, sweets, alcohol, TV, or cigarettes.

Possible Brain Regions Involved
- Left temporal lobe functions creating a sense of a bounded ego, separated from the rest of the brain, from animal instincts, and from nature, mother, or God
- Left-brain linear functions allowed to dominate while right-brain intuitive functions are ignored

You may be lacking the Strongest Self's quality of connection.

Scoring and Identifying Your Self-Management Style

If you recognize yourself in all of the symptoms associated with one problem area or more than fifteen of the twenty-five total symptoms, then you definitely need to read this book and use its exercises.

If you recognize yourself in fewer than three symptoms in one problem area or fewer than fifteen total symptoms, you still can learn skills that will make life easier for you and help you maintain a stable sense of a self that functions at the highest human levels.

If you don't identify with any of the twenty-five symptoms, I'd like to learn from you. Please contact me.

Notice how you talk to yourself when you're trying to motivate yourself. Is your self-management style effective? If not, you could lessen your stress and become more effective in achieving your goals by learning the effective self-manager skills contained throughout this book. In Chapter 4 you'll learn to speak in the voice of your Strongest Self. For now, while you're in step 1, simply work on identifying the words and feelings that are keeping you stuck in ineffective patterns and empty, counterproductive habits.

By first identifying your symptoms, you're starting to use your executive-brain functions and you're awakening your Strongest Self to apply (in step 3) the five qualities that replace those symptoms. You can start today by using the following fear inoculation exercise to help you clearly identify your reactions and break through any blocks to the unlocking of your full potential.

Exercise for Chapter 1: Get Your Fear Inoculation Shot

Begin by choosing three of your most stressful or worrisome tasks in your career or in your personal life right now. Write them down in your notebook.

Next do a mental rehearsal in which you confront one of your most stressful work, relationship, or life situations. See and feel yourself in that scene. Remember, it's essential that you face discomfort, fear, and self-doubt for a few breaths to free yourself of phobias, avoidant behaviors, and destructive habits. Fear that's avoided can turn into a phobia.

- Close your eyes so that you can accurately identify what's happening in your body and mind.
- Notice how you react during the first five seconds. What happens in your body (breathing, heart rate, and areas of muscle tension), your thoughts or images, your feelings? How do you talk to yourself?
- Notice your reactions without making judgments or comparisons. Simply observe and then take note of your automatic reactions to pressure, stress, and confrontation. Again, in a notebook, make note of:

    a. physical sensations
    b. thoughts or images
    c. inner dialogue

Stay with that stressful or overwhelming scene for thirty seconds (that's five to six deep breaths), and you'll earn your fear inoculation shot, helping you become more robust and resilient to stress and fear in the future. When you choose to stay with something you've been avoiding, you're telling your lower brains that the leader has decided to problem solve rather than run away. Your brain and body will shut off the fight-or-flight response and bring you a calmer, more focused level of energy. Take note of any changes you notice in just thirty seconds of mental rehearsal. How did your breathing, heart rate, muscle tension, thoughts, and feelings change?

If your tension increases, read the rest of this chapter and then repeat this exercise from the perspective of an observer. From a distance, observe your physical and emotional reactions, as if watching them on TV or in a movie. If there's no improvement after two to three repetitions, you may be suffering from severe anxiety or post–traumatic stress symptoms and may want to consult with a licensed therapist.

Once you identify your initial reactions to stress and pressure, you'll be prepared to shift to optimal levels of performance, balance, and effectiveness. Instead of being stuck in old habits and fears, you'll be in charge of choosing to act in ways that are congruent with your higher vision and values, and with the full potential of your new, human brain.

Lauren's Fear Inoculation Shot: Taking the Bar Exam

Lauren had failed the state bar exam seven times and was afraid of losing her job if she failed again. Lauren started her mental rehearsal by seeing herself in a large room about to take the three-day exam for the eighth time.

She followed the exercise's instructions to notice how she reacted during the first five seconds. She paid attention—without judgment—to what was happening in her body (her breathing, heart rate, and areas of muscle tension), her thoughts or images, her feelings, and how she talked to herself. Lauren first noticed that her automatic reactions to pressure and stress included muscle tension in her shoulders and neck and tightness in her stomach. Her thoughts and images involved fear of failure, resentment, and embarrassment. She noticed that her initial inner dialogue was made up of thoughts about the future (the wish that this ordeal was over and that she had passed the exam), pressure to do well or else ("I have to pass or else I'll lose my job"), and self-blame and self-criticism ("How did you get into this mess? What's wrong with you?").

Lauren did this exercise several times to get her fear inoculation shots and prepare herself for an optimal performance by first becoming aware of her initial, ineffective reactions. Then she learned how to shift to the perspective of her Strongest Self and replace stress with the quality of safety (even if she failed again) and inner conflict with fully choosing to take the entire three-day exam to demonstrate what she knows.

The part of her that was afraid of failure and resistant to retaking the exam again began to quiet down as Lauren assumed her role as a strong leader. She discovered that she could gain the cooperation of every part of her in confronting a very difficult task and that she could actually enjoy taking the exam—and passing it on her eighth try.

Mental Rehearsal: Confronting Fear and Stress

Repeat the mental rehearsal exercise just described with any of your top three stressful situations every day for *one week*. Soon you'll identify your default or knee-jerk reactions and know when they are most likely to occur. Start with whichever situation you're most comfortable confronting—such as talking to a troublesome neighbor, asking your boss for a raise, or facing your income taxes. As you build confidence, confront the more fearful situations. This will evoke your strongest initial reactions and, therefore, make them easier to identify.

Do a mental rehearsal for any project, person, or situation that evokes anxiety, self-doubt, or avoidance. Identify your initial physical, emotional, and cognitive reactions that occur during the first two to five seconds. This will prepare you to perform optimally in the actual situation.

Stay with the imagined scene and the feelings it evokes for at least thirty seconds—approximately five to six breaths. Confronting it for thirty seconds, without using your usual escape mechanisms, will earn you a fear inoculation shot and prepare you to face future challenges with greater ease. You and your higher brain will begin to take charge of your time and your life.

Shortcut Exercises

During a very good vacation, you hopefully become reacquainted with that part of you that can, without much worry or planning, relax and have a good time. You may discover that you can deal with minor upsets and disappointments without letting them ruin your day.

This is a good time to observe and identify the default fears and habits that can operate like tentacles to pull you back into your prevacation patterns. For one day consider *all* your initial reactions as obsolete, conditioned responses that must be reviewed and updated. Observe them and consider what new options might replace them. You'll find examples of healthier, more effective alternatives in the next three chapters.

Congratulations! You've completed an important and essential first step to getting unstuck from old, debilitating patterns. In the chapters that follow, you'll learn how to replace these empty, outdated habits with the five qualities that will unite all parts of yourself in the achievement of your highest goals and values.

2

Expand Your Identity Beyond Your Ego

No matter what a person's complaint when he has a lesson with me, I have found the most beneficial first step is to encourage him to see and feel what he is doing—that is, to increase his awareness of what actually is.

—Tim Gallwey, *The Inner Game of Tennis*

SPORTS CAN BE a low-risk, fun, and quick way to practice expanding your sense of self beyond your conscious mind, its controllable muscles, and willpower. Learning to improve your golf swing, skating technique, or tennis serve can become the equivalent of a meditation or mindfulness practice. In order to perform optimally in any activity, you must put aside the worries of your ego and its distracting voices while connecting your higher brain to the wisdom of your body. It's this integration with an expanded sense of self that allows us to effortlessly play in the *zone* beyond the ego's struggles and the conscious mind's lack of confidence.

When we confine our sense of identity to our conscious mind and the muscles we can control, we limit ourselves to the brainpower of only the left hemisphere of our brain, which *grasps* linear knowledge. This limited view treats our mind as if it were a controllable muscle and separates us from the wisdom of our larger, subconscious mind—the right brain, our dreaming mind —and our body's intuitive knowledge of mechanics and physics. This concept of grasping information leaves out the ease and power of our right brain, which *opens to absorb* wisdom the way an infant learns language and speech and progresses from crawling to walking at phenomenal rates. Without a fully formed, separated ego to get in its way, the infant's rate of learning is immeasurably faster than that of an egocentric adult, who's overidentified with his or her struggling mind and consciously controlled muscles.

Such a limited sense of identity raises several questions: Who takes care of you when your conscious mind and ego go to sleep? What part of you continues to work—creating dreams, continuing to breathe, and repairing cells, producing more than five million healthy new red blood cells every minute, even though you don't know much about cellular biology or anatomy? How can you expand your identity to include more of your brain-cell power, your subconscious wisdom, and the support of something superior to your ego and beyond the control of your conscious mind? What part of you coordinates and integrates all these diverse functions?

The answers to these questions will become apparent to you as you complete the exercises in steps 1 and 2. In the next few weeks, as you practice the exercises in all four steps to awaken your Strongest Self, you will find that you no longer think of yourself as limited to the reactions of your lower brains, your old habits, or the struggles of some small, separated part of your personality. Instead, you will be able to connect with and use the more expansive wisdom and strength of your Strongest Self and its deeper resources, including the subconscious mind, the integrated left- and right-brain hemispheres, and the wisdom of your body.

You Don't Have to Feel Disconnected

When you identify with just your ego, conscious mind, personality, or lower brain responses, you make yourself more vulnerable to stress, ambivalence, worry, self-doubt, confusion, and fear of criticism and abandonment. From its limited resources, the ego will try hard to manage your life as if it's alone and separate from any support. Trying to cope with life while disconnected from a larger support system also makes it more likely that you will seek to escape from fear and pain through external fixes, such as overeating, abuse of alcohol or drugs, and excessive TV watching or Internet surfing—anything to try to ease the pain of struggling alone.

Shifting your identity to a more expansive self, on the other hand, decreases stress and self-sabotage and your dependency on drugs or relationships by centering your identity in a larger support system and perspective. Your capacity for creativity and productivity are also increased by uniting your conscious mind with the subconscious genius-mind and the left-brain hemisphere with its twin on the right side of the brain.

To learn how the process of connecting to your Strongest Self is radically different from simply pressuring your ego or personality to try harder, you'll need to perform a little experiment.

Essential Exercise for Connecting Beyond Your Ego

It is essential that you complete this exercise if you wish to benefit fully from this program.

1. Stand and hold (in one hand) a book, briefcase, or purse straight out at shoulder height until you feel uncomfortable or tired. Imagine doing this all day, every day, and consider what habits and dependencies you would develop in order to simply cope and survive.

2. Once again, stand and hold the object out in front of you until you feel tired. Then bring your elbow to your hip or side. Now place your other hand underneath the object to support its weight. Notice how much easier it is to hold the same weight when your arm is connected to the rest of your body and gets support from your other hand.

3. For an even greater sense of connection with something beyond your struggling ego, stand with your knees bent and let your hips, legs, and feet sink into the support of the floor. Take a deep breath, hold it, and as you exhale, imagine that you are floating down into the floor, the building, and the earth itself. Your ego, personality, and conscious mind are no longer working and struggling alone. You now are connected to, and held by, the stronger, wiser support system of your body, your integrated brain, and the laws of nature.

The discomfort you felt in the first part of this exercise is analogous to the struggle, fatigue, and pain that you may feel in life when a part of you—represented in this exercise by your extended arm and hand—acts as if it must work alone. By performing this simple exercise, you learn that everything is easier when you connect to the support of your self and whole brain (represented in this exercise by your body and its connection to the floor and the earth).

When you expand your identity beyond the isolated, lesser parts of your personality and ego, you integrate your conscious and subconscious resources, making it easier to face life's challenges from a center of inner peace and support. The same can be said when you expand your resources to include friends and a community that validates your worth and creates an environment in which you are safe to be your true self.

The world-famous psychiatrist and clinical hypnotist Dr. Milton Erickson used to say that much of our fear about life comes from thinking of ourselves as if we were a small cup of water.

From that limited perspective, the loss of just a few drops of water would feel like a serious threat to our identity and security. The late Dr. Erickson would then say, "How different it is to be the ocean! When you're the ocean, they can't hurt you. They can take a whole tub of water from you—and it won't hurt you one bit." Most of our former problems and symptoms diminish when we learn to live from our Strongest—"oceanic"—Self.

Step Out of Your Old Identity

When I was growing up in Jersey City, New Jersey, it was my dream to become an expert skier. But most of my adult life I remained stuck at the intermediate level. Whenever I confronted an expert slope, I would cope by attempting to ski for about fifty yards across the slope at an angle, and then—before picking up too much speed—I would apply the brilliant strategy of falling in order to stop. I would then slide across the slope in the opposite direction, take another strategic fall, and repeat this process until I was down the steepest and iciest part of the mountain. This less-than-dignified way of coping worked, but—as with most primitive methods of coping—it was quite painful, exhausting, and grossly inadequate for confronting the more interesting slopes and rewarding challenges in life.

Don't Wait for the Old You to Feel Confident

On March 12, 1992, at Whistler Mountain, in British Columbia, I was fortunate to meet an extraordinary ski instructor named Wendell, who said two things that would set in motion the work for this book. Wendell looked at his class of ten skiers, all over the age of forty, and said, "You all have the latest equipment that allows you to ski effortlessly. But you're still struggling as if you're using the heavy skis and boots you had when you first started to ski twenty or thirty years ago."

What a perfect metaphor, I thought, for what I see repeatedly in my work with therapy and coaching clients. These are accomplished people, with hard-won skills, but instead of using the new equipment of their competent, adult selves, they approach issues in their lives today from the fears, outdated coping style, and self-doubts that they've been dragging along with them since childhood. They continue to struggle from isolated parts of themselves, with outdated tools, archaic brains, and a very limited perspective.

Shifting to a New Self Is Faster than Changing the Old One

Your identity—who you think you are—is the chief controller of your life. It will determine what you hope for and how you make yourself feel. To reach the full potential and joy of your true, Strongest Self, you must free yourself of your old, limited identity and its primitive ways of coping.

It turned out that Wendell was not only an excellent ski instructor; he was an extraordinary teacher of life skills. His second statement had an even greater impact on me than his first. He said, "I don't have time to teach the *old you* how to ski effortlessly, like an expert. So I'm changing your names to those of natural-born skiers." Pointing to each member of our ski class, he continued, "You can be Fritz; you're Franz. You're Heidi, you're Ingrid; and Neil, you're Jean-Claude Killy, Olympic skier."

By rapidly shifting my identity away from the *old me*, Wendell freed me of my fearful voice and put me into the role and identity of a champion skier—certain of his ability to control both his skis and any self-doubts left over from his past. With Wendell's coaching, and unburdened from my old image of myself, I learned—in just three days—how to ski from the very top of the mountain down slopes marked "for expert skiers only."

On March 15, I pointed my skis directly down the face of that mountain and skied like an expert without once having to fall. I still could hear the old fearful voice with a heavy Jersey City accent shouting, "We're going too fast. I don't know how to ski like this! Where ya gonna fall?" But the thrill of skiing far beyond my usual ability, in a scene of snowcapped mountains and pine trees in every direction, kept me focused on achieving my life-long dream. I wasn't going to allow my old fears to pull me out of this beautiful connection with the mountain, with nature, and with my newfound ability to integrate every part of me.

For the first time in my life, I was skiing effortlessly—my skis carving tight S-patterns all the way down the glacier—faster, straighter, and steeper than I'd ever skied before. Everything seemed to be in slow motion. When I could see my skis carve back and forth beneath my body, I knew that I was in the zone that top athletes talk about—a place of extraordinary perform-ance that far exceeds our ego's expectations and what's possible through conscious effort alone. My mind and body, my conscious and subconscious minds, and the left and right hemispheres of my brain were united.

What I discovered on the slopes that day was quite remarkable. Each of us can make rapid improvements, almost effortlessly, if we do the following:

1. Step out of our old identity and stop struggling from its lim-ited perspective.
2. Step up to an expanded sense of self that has new, improved equipment and access to a new brain with its expansive wis-dom and resources.
3. Shift from initial fears and reactions to focusing on our dreams and mission.
4. Awaken the self in us that unites all parts around the goal of unlocking our full human potential.

Each of us can learn to shift to an updated identity that includes our new brain equipment and allows us to effortlessly perform at levels far beyond the confidence of our old identity.

A Return to Wholeness

In *Transformation*, Robert A. Johnson succinctly states what is at the heart of most of our human worries and struggles: loss of wholeness, unconditional love, and "paradise"; the futile search for paradise in the past and from external objects; and the growing pains of transformation necessary to bring us to wholeness once again.

If you wish to be in charge of your life and reach your full potential, your challenge will be one of going forward from the lost paradise of infancy to a new form of wholeness. One purpose of this book is to provide you with a compass to find your own path to wholeness and to equip you with the tools you'll need to achieve a new sense of self that is integrated and whole.

Much of our discontent today occurs when we allow a small, separated ego part of us to search for that bliss in all the wrong places. This ego part and conscious mind—which feels separated from mother, God, paradise, and the subconscious mind—is simply a fact of our evolutionary history and our process of development. It's not necessarily a problem or a mistake.

Our task is to acknowledge the issue of separation, real or imagined, and to discover the access route to integration and wholeness. In this first step to awaken your Strongest Self, you're learning to recognize when you're reacting to life from a small, primitive part of you. This prepares you to make shifts, in step 2, to the perspective and roles that will facilitate the expansion of your identity into that of a stronger and more whole sense of self.

The following chart contrasts the qualities of those who have shifted their identities from their separated egos to their integrated Strongest Self—connected to its resources and the power of its leadership brain functions and roles. Listed in the left-hand column are the skills you will attain through the daily practice of the exercises and concepts contained in this book. Those who have connected every part of themselves to their Strongest Self, and to the self's own deeper resources, live from a perspective of greater security and less struggle. Those who live from an identity that is simply their ego or personality, separated from their larger self, find themselves struggling alone and using inadequate, primitive mechanisms to cope, as detailed in the right-hand column.

> **Connected or Separated and Struggling?**

When You Are Connected to Your Strongest Self . . .	When You Have a Separated Ego and Are in a Lonely Struggle . . .
You acknowledge and mourn the loss of paradise, unlimited power, and unconditional love.	You deny your loss, maintain the illusion of unlimited power, and feel guilty.
You acknowledge and accept your vulnerability to suffering and loss.	You deny your vulnerability and become extremely anxious about potential losses.
You are self-accepting and forgiving and provide safety from self-threats.	You are self-critical and frequently use self-threatening statements that cause you chronic stress.
You have a clear vision and priorities and keep them congruent with your higher values.	You are distracted by the latest urgency and are always working for some future security.
You guarantee your inner worth, making you safe from judgment.	You allow your worth to be determined by external events, other people, and your performance and achievements.
You have access to inner resources that allow you to perform optimally with ease.	You must struggle because you rely solely on the limited resources of your conscious mind.
You operate from choice, thereby breaking the inner conflict between parts.	You remain immobilized by and ambivalent about the inner conflict between the inner voices of "have to" and "don't want to."

(continued)

When You Are Connected to Your Strongest Self . . .	When You Have a Separated Ego and Are in a Lonely Struggle . . .
You can enjoy the present as a precious moment of life.	You are anxious about the future and regretful of the past.
You work from a win-win perspective that builds relationships and allows for different points of view.	You operate from win-lose, right-wrong thinking that creates arguments and conflict.
You trust in and connect with a deeper wisdom and a strong support system, thereby permitting spontaneity and relaxation.	You need to control outcomes and stay vigilant in order to avoid mistakes and maintain an illusion of security.

Notice which symptoms of the separated, lonely, struggling ego—in the column on the right—best describe your current behavior patterns. Then study the qualities in the left-hand column, which you'll be gaining as you learn to connect with your Strongest Self.

Marie: Committing to Her New Identity

A coaching client named Marie wanted help in dealing with feeling overwhelmed by the demands of her new, rapidly growing business. At the age of forty-two, Marie had achieved her dream of having her own business, but her rapid success began to take over her life, causing her to feel stressed and anxious. She said, "I've lost control of my life and my time. I want to be more focused on my top priorities, my health and my family."

Within a few sessions Marie grasped the concepts that I have been describing and practiced the exercise at the end of this chapter both on the job and at home. To remind herself of her ability to shift from an overwhelmed, frantic part of herself to her new identity as her Strongest Self, Marie composed a list of "I" statements. She posted the following list on the refrigerator, the bathroom mirror, and all over her office:

- *I* am now the one who listens to all the parts that make up my total self.
- *I* no longer allow the overwhelmed part of me to struggle alone, worrying about how to manage my life.
- *I* don't want the inmates running the asylum. *I* don't want the players telling the coach how they'll play the game.
- *I* now have a team of players to unite around *my* higher goals.
- *I* am now the one who must apologize to the childlike parts of me for not taking responsibility for my life sooner.
- *I* am now the one who shows up to do the job of directing my life.
- *I* now catch the smaller parts of me before they sink into old stories and patterns and try to cope alone with overwhelming projects.
- *I* am my Strongest Self, connected to a still stronger and deeper wisdom.

Marie no longer identifies solely with the ego part of her that thinks it must struggle as if isolated and alone. When she becomes aware of feeling overwhelmed, she uses that awareness as a signal to wake up her Strongest Self to take charge and provide support. She's learned that it's a waste of time to try to tackle her work projects and personal issues from the limited identity and resources of a small part of herself. Several times a day, when Marie faces stressors, she notices them as the extended arm in the essential exercise discussed earlier and reminds herself to exhale into the support of the chair and floor and connect with her expanded sense of self.

This new ability would be sufficient to free Marie from her old patterns and allow her to work and live more joyfully and productively. But what brings her an even greater sense of inner peace, she says, is the feeling that her newly awakened Strongest Self is connected to, and supported by, an even deeper wisdom, or higher power.

Exercise for Chapter 2: You Are Not Alone

You are beginning to expand your sense of self to include both your conscious and subconscious skills. Now you can use the symptoms of struggle and worry as alarms that warn you to catch some separated part of you from trying to cope with your life from its limited and lonely perspective. Managing your life from such a limited part of you is no longer necessary or acceptable. It's not as effective or energy efficient as operating from a self that integrates all parts in pursuit of your higher values and objectives. The following exercise will help you shift your identity to your Strongest Self and away from the small, separated parts of you that continue in the same old rut of trying to run your life with outdated skills.

1. For one week, notice any physical or emotional struggle as a sign that you are trying to work from a small part of yourself, separated from the support of your body and Strongest Self. To recall how that feels, repeat the earlier essential exercise of holding a book, cup, or briefcase out at arm's length.
2. Observe and catch yourself saying or thinking, "*I* am depressed, frightened, overwhelmed, or stressed."
3. When you notice that you're identifying with a small part of you (possibly from the past), quickly replace your initial words and thoughts with, "A *part* of me feels depressed, frightened, overwhelmed, or stressed" or "Now I'm aware of feelings of stress, depression, etc."

This exercise will help you disidentity from your ego's outmoded coping patterns and your lower brain's reactive habits that have kept you from realizing your true potential. This practice will allow you to maintain your commitment to living from your larger, Strongest Self and your higher values. Now you're prepared for step 2, the process of shifting to the perspective, roles, and voice of your more robust, wiser Strongest Self.

Step Up to Your New Brain and Your Strongest Self

3

Step Up to Your Strongest Self's Point of View

The subjective sense . . . of possessing . . . inner serenity . . . is, in fact, often accompanied by a feeling that there is something superior to the ego, something which is, as it were, directing the course of the individual's development.

—Anthony Storr, *The Integrity of the Personality*

IN 1980 PEGGY STARTED WORKING with me in order to advance in her career, but she found herself stuck in a tug-of-war between two inner voices—one that was afraid of failure and an opposing one that was critical and bullying. At that time, I was using a Gestalt therapy technique in which clients change chairs whenever they take on the voice and perspective of a different part of themselves. As Peggy changed chairs and took on the perspective of each side of the inner conflict, she could see how the battle between two aspects of her feelings and thoughts was keeping her stuck. From my third perspective, the therapist's chair, I wrote down the dialogue between the two sides of the conflict while keeping Peggy's goals in mind.

It occurred to me that if Peggy took my therapist's chair, she could gain the benefit of a third perspective, similar to the observing and decision-making functions of the human prefrontal cortex. When she sat in my chair, I moved between the two seats of the conflicting parts and read back what was said when she had taken on their perspectives and voices. This adjustment to the Gestalt technique brought about an unexpected rapid and positive shift in Peggy's attitude and confidence level.

Seeing things from a third perspective, Peggy easily assumed the role of an empowered and compassionate leader. She then could be more objective, see alternatives, and remember her commitment to *her* goals rather than remaining caught in the fears and squabbling of her inner voices. Peggy's shift parallels what happens when we awaken our Strongest Self and its executive organizing functions.

Once outside the smaller perspectives of her lower brains, Peggy could hear their fears and conflicts and realize that they had taken control of her life. Now, instead of being caught up in their arguing, she could soothe the fears of one part while relaxing the zeal and worries of the opposing side.

Discovering a Third Perspective

The third-chair technique, as Peggy named it, is a physical representation of what happens when we observe our inner voices and reactions and unite them around the top point of a triangle or phalanx. A leader—the human part of your brain—has shown up, provided a clear direction, and integrated all members in a cooperative effort. Without exception, all clients who have shifted to the third-chair perspective have changed their physical posture and voice, assumed a leadership role, and, in effect, said to the other parts of themselves: "You guys have been ruining my life. I need you to cooperate with my goals. I'm tired of being stuck in the same old, self-defeating rut. Now I am in charge."

Peggy discovered that as she took on adult responsibility for facing her fears, her frightened voices lowered their volume, making it possible for her to achieve her dream of completing college and building a very successful career in a field that she loves. She no longer stays stuck in inner conflict but uses her awareness of the ambivalence and conflict to awaken her Strongest Self, shift perspective, and offer every part of her nonjudgmental, therapeutic acceptance regardless of what happens.

The third-chair technique, though developed twenty-five years ago, retains its power to facilitate the essential shift into the third perspective of a wise, Strongest Self—capable of breaking the tug-of-war between conflicted inner parts. In Peggy's case it was noteworthy that the third chair was a therapist's chair—representing a role that acts as an accepting and compassionate container for all parts of us and all aspects of the human drama with all its sorrows, joys, and potential.

The Power of Roles to Change Our Perspective

Taking charge of our lives and making of them what we desire means letting go of old baggage and redefining ourselves in terms of who we wish to be—integrated with our adult skills, objectives, and challenges. As I now tell my seminar participants, you don't have time to wait for the old you to feel confident, motivated, or all-knowing. Facing today's challenges requires that you make a leadership decision to show up and start working, in spite of the fact that a part of you has self-doubts, a lack of confidence, or a fear of criticism. When you step into a self-leadership role to take charge of your life, you'll not have the luxury of self-pity or cursing over spilled milk. Before you can finish cursing about some problem—in less time than you need to take one full breath —you'll be focused on the solution. Now *that's* effective time management! Performing at your best—in sports, on work projects, or in relationships—boils down to the same skill: the ability to awaken your mature, Strongest Self so it can unite every part of your brain and psyche in a commitment to achieve your highest values and goals. From this larger sense of self you access cognitive abilities—left brain and right—that are not available to lower functions; a project manager's overview perspective; the ability to negotiate with and gain the cooperation of all aspects of yourself; and the calm and focus of being in the peak performance zone.

Cultures use rituals and initiation rites such as graduation ceremonies, bar and bat mitzvahs, weddings, and inaugurations to facilitate the transition from childhood to adulthood and from simple roles to more complex roles. These rituals help the initiates get unstuck from the past, transcend their old identity, and transform themselves into a new identity with greater authority and responsibility. The coronation ceremony of a king or queen, for example, symbolizes the transformation of an ordinary person into one who must make regal decisions—shifting from the perspective of a little self, responsible only for his or her individual well-being, to that of a larger self, responsible for the welfare of a country. In Great Britain the future monarch is dressed in the costume of a peasant and lies prostrate, as if dead, before the archbishop. The initiate king or queen is anointed and is asked to rise up—as if awakening to a new life and a new role—and accept the crown and scepter as symbols of his or her larger role and powers that support the new identity.

The power of a role, a title, or an office to endow an ordinary person with the authority of a president, king, queen, pope, or chairperson is recognized by the phrase *speaking ex cathedra*, meaning to speak from the official chair or throne. When we speak from the authority granted by our role as a leader in society, we are empowered to make decisions and perform acts that are beyond the capabilities and confidence of our former self. At such times we must invoke the power that comes through us from our office, our seat in government, or our roles as parents and citizens.

In similar fashion your identity is transformed when you take on the role of a protective self toward the more vulnerable parts of yourself. Instead of identifying with only the parts of you that are in conflict, you learn to shift your identity to that of your Strongest Self, setting a clear leadership vision that unites all parts around your current goals and values. From that perspective and role, you can bring into your life the leadership that had been missing. Finally, an adult has shown up to unite all aspects of you and connect them with your adult powers.

The Actor's Exercise: Changing Roles

Society's rituals and ceremonies help us graduate to roles at higher levels of performance and responsibility. But as demonstrated in this actor's exercise, you also can choose which roles to play and which story to tell yourself about who you are. This exercise will help you change roles, perspectives, and moods the way you might if you were an actor and will make you aware of the power of roles to quickly expand your sense of self. While you're acting in a particular role, you take on the perspective and identity of that role, but it's only a temporary identity. It's like changing your clothes from business to casual or experimenting with a new haircut. Inside that new outfit and new look, you feel like a new person, a different version of some essential you. The self inside that role and suit, however, remains the same. The characters you play in your dreams are all parts of you and come from the same essential self.

Your First Role

Imagine that you're an actor who's been playing the part of a depressed, down-and-out person for a year. From the first moment you walk on to the stage—before you say a single word —the audience knows that you're depressed and exhausted. They see you dragging your feet as you move across the stage, your shoulders bowed and head hung low as if you're carrying a heavy burden.

You've played the role so many times that it's hard for you to shift out of the role and back to your usual self. It's as if the depressed character in the play has taken over your life. You embody your character's life story so well that even the other actors and your friends have begun to treat you as someone who is depressed and hopeless. Problem is, the play is closing tonight and you must prepare for a new role.

Your Second Role

Tomorrow you audition for the role of a very successful, confident person who bounces back from the greatest of life's difficulties. In this role you are the exact opposite of your depressed role. The way you enter a room, greet others, and are alert to the beauty in the world all signal that you're very much alive and comfortable with yourself. It wouldn't matter if you were fifty pounds overweight or had a severe handicap; in this role you are connected to some deeper strength that gives you charisma and confidence. People are glad to see you because your joy is infectious and generously shared. They greet you the way a grandparent greets a beloved grandchild or the way a fan looks up to a pop star or an athlete.

Note: The actual events and history for each role—depressed or joyful—can be exactly the same, the only difference being that in the second role you have taken every disastrous event of your life and made it into a stepping-stone to a new level of strength. Instead of identifying yourself as a failure because of losses, negative events, and disappointments, you've seen them simply as facts rather than as evidence that there's something wrong with you. From a higher perspective, you've found a way to accept yourself and to forgive yourself for being human and then moved on. Every difficulty in life has cemented your connection to the support of your Strongest Self.

- **Physical change.** Notice how you must change your body and posture in order to shift from the depressed role to the joyful, energized role. Experiment with trying to have a depressing thought and feeling while you hold your head up and shoulders back and put a smile on your face. Write down your observations in your notebook.

- **Emotional change.** Notice how your feelings change as you let go of the depressive life story and take on the inner dialogue and script of a successful, confident person. Notice the change from fatigue and low motivation to high energy as you shift to a view of a life with possibilities and the resources to confront any challenge. Write down what you experience.

- **Inner dialogue change.** Notice how differently you talk to yourself in the role of a depressed character as opposed to the supportive, encouraging inner dialogue of a joyful person. Develop the thoughts and words of self-support that fit the inner dialogue of a cheerful, effective, hopeful person. If you were that character, how would your parents have talked to you, and how would you talk to yourself, after a loss or failure? What inner dialogue would help you to recover from a tragedy and move on with your life? How would you talk to yourself about your achievements and success? Write down your thoughts and your new inner dialogue.

Michael: Accessing the Roles of the Self

A new, demanding job caused Michael at age forty-two to revert to his old ways of coping: smoking two to three packs of cigarettes and drinking five to ten cups of coffee each day just to keep functioning and then throwing back a double scotch each night to unwind from the stress. Michael knew that he couldn't continue to cope by simply putting in more time and self-medicating with nicotine, caffeine, and alcohol, but he didn't know how to change. All he knew how to do was to push himself harder and harder—starting to work earlier and finishing later. In the three years since Michael started his new business, he had stopped exercising and had gained sixty pounds. By age forty-five Michael already felt like an old man, and yet he kept pushing himself to do what he told himself he simply *had* to do.

All that changed when Michael suffered a heart attack and went through triple bypass surgery. Suddenly, all the things he thought he absolutely *had* to do—and all the to-do list tasks that *had* to be finished by the deadline—somehow got done without him or simply faded away. Motivated by this major health crisis and by the hope that there was a better way to live, Michael followed a friend's advice to call me for an appointment. When I described the Awaken Your Strongest Self program, Michael initially didn't believe he had a self that could act as a calm, protective center for him. But once he started the first step of observing and identifying his initial reactions to stress, Michael discovered that he could gain some control and lower his stress level.

Within weeks of starting the process, Michael was eager to move on to step 2, where he'd learn to work with greater ease from the perspective, roles, and voice of the self. Because he is the owner of a business and is responsible for the jobs of thirty people, Michael decided that he would cast his Strongest Self in the role of the enlightened manager.

As Michael took on this role, he noticed that he was able to put aside his old, pushy style, one that he initially defended as being unchangeable because it was simply his nature. From this new perspective, he was now able to communicate a new message to his body—one of safety rather than chronic threats to his worth, life, and future success. He was now listening to his body and directing its energy into what he called "a coherent laser focus that gets the job done without unnecessary stress." His enlightened management style made him feel more flexible and relaxed when mistakes happened. Both he and his employees were less stressed and worried. As a result, they made fewer errors, and when corrections were necessary, they made them more quickly.

For most people, finding the motivation to change their unhealthy habits requires a tough journey of discipline and years of commitment to therapy or a spiritual or religious practice. Yet for others, like Michael, it seems to happen instantly after they've faced a crisis or survived a near-death experience. When psychiatrists David Raft, M.D., and Jeffrey Andresen, M.D., studied nineteen patients who recovered after clinically dying for a few minutes during heart surgery, they found remarkable changes in their patients' personalities. This group of survivors became "very curious about themselves . . . and achieved changes that bore a striking resemblance to certain changes induced in people by psycho-analysis . . . [but] these survivors . . . apparently grasped the nature of these methods in but a few moments of time—in fact, in the duration of their brush with death." Some discovered new aspects of themselves and learned to incorporate these new aspects into a larger and more comprehensive definition of self. One patient, who had survived cardiac arrest during surgery, spoke of "finding parts of himself that had been lost." Others acquired an increased sense of worth and discovered a new capacity to console themselves about past losses.

Experiencing a crisis or a near-death experience forces us to access resources in our mind and body that are beyond what our conscious mind or ego can do alone. Luckily, you don't need a near-death experience to awaken curiosity and meaning in your life or to learn how to create a sense of safety and self-worth. Nor do you need a crisis to find and integrate lost parts of yourself. By using the Awaken Your Strongest Self program, you are learning how to achieve these results without having to experience a life-threatening crisis.

Exercise for Chapter 3: Choosing Your Role

Consider how Michael initially didn't believe any program could help him, and yet he was very successful in improving his life once he took the first steps in this process. Michael chose the role of the enlightened manager as one he could relate to and aspire to. What role would help you shift to a larger, more robust sense of self?

Continue to identify your initial reactions and default patterns. Use your awareness of a reactive pattern to remind you to exhale and say "Stop" to yourself as you shift to the perspective and role of your larger self. Use the following three steps throughout this process to shift to your larger self:

1. Notice the initial reactions of the fearful, self-doubting, overwhelmed parts of you. Notice them as just *parts* of a larger you—a larger whole self.
2. From your place of noticing, validate—with compassion and understanding—the fears and self-doubts of every part of you with a "yes" and a statement as described in the discussion on the voice of the self in Chapter 4.
3. Start taking charge of one aspect of your life—managing your reactions to stress, for example. Empowered by your new role as a self-leader, assert a compelling vision that will unite all parts of you in achieving your higher values and goals.

In my early research for this book, I personally interviewed or gathered questionnaire responses from more than one hundred individuals who positively transformed their lives after a crisis, an illness, an accident, or a near-death experience. When I analyzed the qualities that had been awakened in these individuals, I discovered that five qualities stood out as the main contributors to inner peace and strength. These five qualities—the qualities of your Strongest Self—are safety, choice, presence, focus, and connection. The next chapter provides an introduction to these qualities, which you will then practice at length in Chapters 5 through 9. These qualities are based on the strengths and insights gained by individuals who, in the process of surviving overwhelming challenges, awakened their Strongest Selves to play a leadership role in their lives.

4

Speak Up in the Voice of Your Strongest Self

I treat myself as I treat a child I love. In respecting him [or her], I dignify all aspects of the human condition. . . . I bring no harsh judgment to him. In accepting all that he is, he need not fear me. . . . Thus, we exist in a state of grace, in a state relatively free of the tensions and fears born of chronic impending destructive judgment, criticism, and castigation.

> —Theodore Rubin, *Compassion and Self-Hate: An Alternative to Despair*

IN 1980 I HAD THE PRIVILEGE of speaking at the first Mind–Brain Conference, in San Francisco, with seven hundred scientists, physicians, researchers, and therapists in attendance. Unlike most of the speakers, I had no slides of the brain or lists of hormones released during a stress response, and I didn't have "scientific" research to prove the effectiveness of my clinical methods. Therefore, I felt a bit intimidated. But that didn't stop me from taking the bold step of engaging this science-oriented audience in a relaxation and imagery exercise to demonstrate how quickly they could quiet their body's stress response. I hoped that their subjective experience would serve as evidence that the mind can calm the body and gain its cooperation with messages of safety.

I asked each member of the audience to imagine a stressful situation and then note which symptoms of stress—muscle tension, upset stomach, shallow breathing, sweaty palms, rapid heartbeat—arose for them. I then asked them to notice how rapidly they could lower their stress level by consciously exhaling, making a decision about their level of safety, and giving themselves messages of acceptance rather than worry. In the middle of this exercise, a man rose from the back of the ballroom and began shouting his disagreement with my methods as he marched to the exit, where he hurled his last invective as he slammed the door.

Fortunately, I barely noticed his remarks because I was intensely focused on my job of completing the relaxation imagery for the audience, and I had imagined a protective atmosphere (an exercise included later in this chapter) all around me to buffer any concerns that might cause stress. On hearing the man's insults, I thought, "Normally, that kind of attack would have bothered me. But this time I'm not taking his words personally. I must be in an altered state, a protective zone. This stuff really works!"

How to Access the Voice of Your Strongest Self

I didn't have time to deal with the man's attitude or to take his remarks personally; I had a job to do. So I continued with the exercise, completed my presentation, and found that most of the audience seemed to stay focused as well. Nevertheless, on the following Saturday, I nervously waited for the mail to see the audience's evaluations of my presentation. I quickly turned to the ten most critical evaluations and spent more than two hours of my sunny weekend trying to figure out how to please these critics who felt my presentation was too psychological and too touchy-feely for them.

During those two hours my Strongest Self was asleep. Some part of me that feared criticism and needed to please everyone had taken control of *my* precious weekend. This part was like a child reaching out to a parent and pleading, "Please love me. I need your unconditional acceptance." It was seeking a return to what Robert A. Johnson calls "humanity's original wholeness . . . by going back to an earlier stage of consciousness."

My adult self knows better than to seek the paradise of unconditional love in the past. But my Strongest Self had to be awakened before it could catch the vulnerable part of myself and prevent it from keeping me stuck in an old pattern of trying to return to the infant's Garden of Eden, where love and approval are easily given. It wasn't until my Strongest Self was finally awakened that I could observe the child in me with compassion—and I was able to view the evaluations more objectively. Finally, I could see that more than six hundred people really liked what I had to say. In fact, the audience ranked me third out of twelve speakers, among them some excellent science teachers and researchers.

Rather than analyze why some part of me was so vulnerable to criticism and sought universal acceptance, I simply acknowledged that it *is* a part of me. While I was shocked to find that this childlike reaction was still strong enough to pull me into its primitive fears and away from my current adult goals and skills, I was grateful for the opportunity to integrate it with my Strongest Self. With the executive functions of my brain now in charge, I could focus my attention on the 98 percent of the audience who felt that the psychological nature of my presentation was exactly what they needed. This vast majority appreciated that the imagery exercises and the emotional involvement of the audience added balance to the mostly scientific presentations of the Mind-Brain Conference.

The "Yes" Template

By observing the reactions of the approval-seeking part of me and labeling them as incongruent with my adult strengths and objectives, I was able to choose how to respond. Knowing that I had access to the alternative perspective of my Strongest Self, I could shift to a protective role toward this dependent and primitive part of me and provide it with an *inner* acceptance that cannot be attained from external approval or achievements. Shifting to the voice of the self, I could offer compassion to the child that I was and understanding to the lower brain survival functions that cause the child to seek approval. Using the "yes" template (which you'll also use in Chapters 5 through 9), I imagined speaking to a child and saying:

- *Yes*, that really hurt you.
- *Yes, of course* you want their approval, just as at an earlier time in your life you needed the approval of your mother and father to survive. (All mammal infants are naturally dependent on adults for survival and are hardwired to seek their attention and approval.)
- *Yes*, you want to convince the critics that you're willing to change in order to win their approval. (We are hardwired by survival instincts to submit to authorities and to blame ourselves rather than to see their inadequacies.)
- *And now I'm choosing* to join the vast majority of the audience that applauded and really liked what we did. I don't want to spend my weekend feeling upset about criticism or rejection by less than 2 percent of the audience. You don't have to deal with this alone. (When you awaken your Strongest Self, no part of you has to act alone or take full responsibility for running your life.)
- Now there's a Strongest Self here that can stand up and speak up for you. I won't allow the critics to judge your worth. Your worth is safe with me. (Safety, acceptance, and protection now come from inside you. Your integrated self is less dependent on external fixes.)
- I'm so sorry to see you seeking acceptance from critics who can't give it and who you can't fix or convince to change. (In the real world we must mourn our losses and acknowledge the limits of our power to heal or fix others.)

- It's over. I'm letting go of trying to fix a problem from the past. I can accept you even though you no longer are the powerful infant who could make everybody happy. It's not your fault that things have changed. It's just part of growing up. (The positive side of mourning and letting go of trying to solve problems from the past is that you find self-acceptance in the present.)

This format ("Yes . . . yes, of course . . . yes . . . and now I'm choosing what to do") calls for at least three validations of your initial responses, emotions, and beliefs before linking the past to the present (with "and now"). In the present moment your Strongest Self is awake and capable of taking responsibility for appraising threats and regulating lower brain (especially amygdala and reptile brain) fear reactions. It is the awakened self that will choose how to act in alignment with your current goals, challenges, and capabilities.

Since that Saturday when I was overwhelmed by a more dependent part of myself, I no longer waste time trying to please everyone in the audience to the detriment of those who want to hear my message. As you learn to speak in the voice of your Strongest Self, I'm sure you'll find that you no longer have to wait for all the parts of you to feel accepted, perfect, confident, or motivated before you can choose to act in ways consistent with your adult skills and objectives.

Exercise: Create a Protective Atmosphere

I'd like you to experience the safe feelings that your Strongest Self can provide you in times of stress. I invite you to imagine that you have your own protective atmosphere four feet all around you. By creating a visual-sensory image, you are communicating in a voice that speaks more effectively to the right hemisphere and to the limbic-emotional center of your brain. With the right brain awake and ready to assist, your left brain—considered to be the center of language and ego identity—can relax its vigilance and lonely struggle.

Allow the image of the atmosphere and your body's ever-present defenses to protect you, so your consciously controlled muscular and nervous system can take a brief vacation. The calming effect that results will prepare you for the task of assuming the role, words, and voice of your Strongest Self.

- Think of a safe, protective scene in nature or at home where you can feel at peace with the world. As you relax within this sanctuary, consider the fact that your mind and body know how to make more than five million healthy new red blood cells every minute—that your body and its autonomic nervous system take care of you twenty-four hours a day, even when the conscious part of you goes to sleep.
- Imagine, feel, and sense a protective atmosphere all around you, a protective bubble in which you feel very comfortable. Like the earth's atmosphere, it weighs 14.7 pounds per square inch at sea level—thick enough to burn up most meteorites before they reach you and yet porous enough to allow you to breathe easily.
- Fill your protective field with a golden or white light that burns up negative thoughts and noises before they get to your heart. Your atmosphere slows down the daily intrusions of life and gives you all the time you need to push distractions aside, find the right words to address problems, and direct your focus on your top priorities. Close your eyes and see, feel, or sense your protective atmosphere all around you.
- Before attempting to go into an interview, make a difficult phone call, confront an angry client, or begin a challenging task, take one to two minutes to feel this warm cocoon of light all around you. Imagine that your protective atmosphere provides you with a center of safety and calm. In the midst of a typically stressful environment, your imagery of a strong, protective bubble makes you appear like the calm at the eye of a tornado. It also sends a message to your lower brain functions—for example, the hippocampus, where memories of former experiences are stored

—that your higher brain has assessed the current environment as safe and one that you can comfortably handle.

Within your atmosphere, you have enough time to observe your conditioned reactions and catch them before they act out their survival programming. You have time to access the voice of your Strongest Self, apply your version of the "yes" template, and stay focused on your job and mission. You'll discover—as I did during my presentation to seven hundred people at the Mind-Brain Conference—that when you integrate all parts of your brain (left with right hemisphere, conscious with subconscious, and new, human brain with lower brains), you create a protective zone that allows you to perform optimally under pressure.

Connect Your Old Identity to Your Strongest Self

Author Robert Bly, in telling of his extraordinary sixtieth birthday party that included friends and celebrities from all around the world, provides us with a creative example of how to speak in the voice of the self. At that time, his book *Iron John* was a bestseller and Bill Moyers had interviewed him on PBS. He should have been on top of the world. But Bly's wife noticed him standing off to the side looking depressed and said, "Robert, all these people are here for your birthday and you look so sad."

With his wife's help, Bly realized what had happened. Memories of depressive scenes from childhood had pulled him back into the identity of a ten-year-old boy who was saying, "No one ever had a birthday party for *me*." At that moment, Bly's adult achievements and successes seemed less real than the familiar feelings of sadness held by the child he had been decades before. With his Strongest Self now awakened to this repeated pattern, Bly was able to dialogue with the image of his boyhood self. He said to that part of him that remained stuck in the past, "Come and be with me at *this* party. I'm here for you now."

A few minutes later his wife returned and noticed how Bly's mood had improved. She said, "Robert, you're back." Indeed, he was back—back from the sadness of his past and back to being his Strongest Self in the role of a protector and guide to the child he once was. By stepping back and observing the depressed feelings of his childhood, Bly was able to assume a protective role that empowered him to shift to the identity of his Strongest Self and its adult strengths.

Neuroscientists and cognitive-behavioral therapists might say that he used his higher executive functions to desensitize a painful memory held in the midbrain's amygdala—an almond-sized organ in the center of the brain that, along with the hippocampus, reacts to, and holds memories of, emotionally charged events.

Notice that Bly's effective process involved listening to his childhood feelings—as in the validating portion of the "yes" template—and then connecting them to his present, Strongest Self. Notice that he didn't try to dismiss or diminish the feelings of sadness with positive statements that would invalidate the pain that *was* real and remains real for the part of him stuck in memories from the distant past. To keep the fears and wounds of the past from undermining the celebration of your current life, you must connect them to the support of your Strongest Self in the present. If left untreated, they can turn into phobias that imprison you in a smaller and smaller life. Your Strongest Self provides a larger container for life's highs and lows, stretching your capability for living a fuller, more joyful life. As one client put it, "I never cried so much or laughed so much as I have this past year. My emotions have been stretched so I can hold more of life's sorrows and life's joys."

The Five Qualities of Your Strongest Self

People who have attained a sense of peace with themselves and the world do not struggle using only their ego, willpower, or conscious intellect. They have learned to awaken their Strongest Self through a daily practice of reconnecting to a center of calm whenever distractions, pressure, or stress pulls them off balance.

Those who awaken their Strongest Self and its higher brain functions exhibit five main qualities:

1. **Safety** within themselves
2. **Choice** of actions that are congruent with their higher values
3. **Presence** in the moment rather than regrets about the past or anticipation of the future
4. **Focus** on what can be done rather than on self-blame for loss or misfortune
5. **Connection** to the deeper resources and support of the larger self that results in ease rather than lonely struggle

How Your Strongest Self Replaces Symptoms with Solutions

The following Rapid Refocusing chart gives you a visual image of five major symptoms and the solutions or qualities that you can exercise to rapidly replace them.

The voice of the Strongest Self can be used to address each of the five major symptoms or problem areas you commonly face in

Rapid Refocusing

From Symptoms		To Solutions and Qualities of the Self
stress and fear	→	safety
inner conflict and procrastination	→	choice
feeling overwhelmed and confused	→	presence
self-criticism and self-blame	→	focus
struggle and loneliness	→	connection

life. These symptoms and problems are not signs that there's anything wrong with you. They simply are what all humans face because our brains contain several ancestral levels and two hemispheres. By learning to recognize these normal symptoms and to replace them with the qualities of your Strongest Self, you'll be shifting to your higher brain and rapidly exercising your truly human talents of choice and adaptation to your current environment.

Please note that these examples are not affirmations that a frightened part of you says to itself. They are messages that your mature self sends to those aspects of you that—without the leadership of your human brain—would be caught in endless loops of worry and stress. When you speak from the perspective and voice of your Strongest Self, you are taking another step in learning to shift out of a limited ego identity and into the identity of a robust self that's supported by deep, inner resources.

The following examples show how the voice of the self can respond to specific symptoms and problems. First use the examples I provide, and then adapt them to fit you, making sure the responsibility for action and change rests with your Strongest Self, not the part that is overwhelmed or frightened.

1. In response to stress and fear. The comforting voice of the Strongest Self creates an atmosphere of safety.

Safety. "Yes, you're afraid and worried. Yes, of course you don't know how to calm yourself. Yes, you're worried that something awful might happen. And now I'm here; you're not alone. I won't let this be the end of the world for us. Your worth is safe with me. I'm strong enough to accept our human vulnerability. Regardless of what happens, I will not make you feel bad. You're safe with me. I will never abandon you."

2. In response to inner conflict and procrastination. The Strongest Self breaks through inner conflict by using the leadership function of choice—a third perspective that is neither "don't want to" nor "have to." This evolved ability to choose, rather than just to react, only exists in your awakened human brain.

Choice. "Yes, this isn't what you'd want to do if you were all-powerful and in total control. Yes, of course you get upset when you don't get what you want. Yes, you don't want to do things that feel uncomfortable. That's normal. And now I choose to face your pain, fear, and lack of confidence in order to avoid greater pain and to achieve my higher goals. I can choose to accept the reality of limited, human control and the consequences of my choices. I can choose to take risks."

3. In response to feeling overwhelmed and confused. The Strongest Self brings the time-traveling mind into the present—the only time and place we can be effective.

Presence. "Yes, you want to do it all and think you should be able to do it all. Yes, you don't want to accept human limits. Yes, it's difficult for you to let go of good things. And now I'm here in the real world of limited time, limited energy, and limited resources. I accept that I can't do it all and that, as a human being, I must live in the present. I choose to let go of the imaginary future and past so I can savor this moment and be effective now."

4. In response to self-criticism and self-blame. The Strongest Self directs our focus toward the task and problem solving and away from self-criticism and self-blame.

Focus. "Yes, you feel bad about what happened. Yes, of course you don't know how to do this job, and you blame yourself. You're wondering, 'What's wrong with me?' Fortunately, you don't have to know everything immediately and you don't need to deal with this task alone. Now I'm here, ready to focus on what we *do know* and *can do now*. Show up and watch for the surprise."

5. In response to struggle and loneliness. The Strongest Self catches and connects with the separated, struggling ego and lets it know it's not alone.

Connection. "Yes, you've learned to struggle alone in order to survive. Yes, of course it's lonely and overwhelming to work so hard alone. Yes, you feel insecure and lack confidence. And now you're no longer alone. I know better than anyone else how hard you've tried and how much you achieved—seemingly, alone. Yes, I know it's hard for you to trust that there's any support beyond your own struggles. Soon you'll discover that when you let go of trying so hard, there's a safety net of support to hold you. I apologize for letting you, my ego and my personality, take so much responsibility for my life. Now I'm here, showing up as the leader of an integrated team effort, determined to use more of my brain-cell power. It's going to be interesting to see how much easier life can be, when you connect to your support system in your larger, Strongest Self."

In steps 1 and 2 of the Awaken Your Strongest Self program, you identified your usual reactive patterns, and in step 3 you can apply the five qualities and roles of your Strongest Self to resolve and replace those patterns. The five qualities and five roles listed in the following chart will empower you to take charge of your life from the perspective of your Strongest Self.

▶ How the Five Qualities and Roles Work

Problem	Quality	Role of the Self	Enhances
stress	**safety**	protector	calm, peace
inner conflict	**choice**	negotiator	motivation, decisiveness
feeling overwhelmed	**presence**	leader	effectiveness, productivity
self-criticism	**focus**	teacher	performance
struggle	**connection**	coach	ease, creativity

These five major problems are caused, in large part, by identifying solely with lower brain reflexes and the ego's conditioned mind, separated from the newly evolved integrating functions of the human brain. There are many more difficulties in life, but these five—stress, inner conflict, feeling overwhelmed, self-criticism, and struggle—are a summary of the major problem areas that thousands of patients and clients have brought to me over the last twenty-five years.

Feel free to expand these problem areas to include the specific problems in your life. For example, the problem area *stress* can include anxiety, worry, and fear; *inner conflict* includes indecisiveness, procrastination, and some forms of depression; *feeling overwhelmed* includes workaholism, lack of confidence, and perfectionism; *self-criticism* includes despair, self-hatred, and self-blame; and *struggle* includes burnout, addictive habits as an attempted escape, and loneliness. Use this list to identify your problem areas and to link them to the qualities and roles of the self that will replace your negative patterns.

Christina: Discovering Her Own Voice

Christina, a mother of two young children, was usually shy and unassertive in most public situations. But whenever her children seemed to be in danger, she would instantly become like a fierce and determined lioness. Christina found that assuming the voice and stance of a protective mama lion toward her adventurous and vulnerable cubs helped her shift into the role of her empowered self.

Drawing on her experiences with rapid shifts from shyness into a maternal protective role, Christina began to choose when to act in the role of a strong, protective self toward those aspects of herself that remained vulnerable to fear and dependency. Now she keeps handy that feeling of being Mama Lion guarding her cubs whenever she notices symptoms of fear or shyness.

Exercise for Chapter 4: Speaking in Your New Compassionate Voice

Decide on an empowering role and voice that fits you and your life situation and connects you with your Strongest Self. You can use as examples Michael's role of an enlightened manager—a role and voice appropriate for him as the owner of a business—or Christina's role as a lioness protective of her cubs. Notice how the voice of your Strongest Self helps you address the needs that underlie each of the five main symptoms and problem areas.

1. Read the earlier examples of the voice of the Strongest Self aloud, and consider recording them. You may find that hearing yourself offering acceptance, comfort, protection, and direction satisfies a long-standing need that former patterns and attempted solutions couldn't adequately address.

2. Notice how hearing supportive phrases in your own voice provides feelings of safety, acceptance, and connection that parts of you have been missing for years or even decades. Because we seldom hear positive and supportive statements coming from ourselves, this pleasant surprise may cause profound feelings of sadness for what you've been missing, as well as calm and relief.

3. Repeat the words of the self—in a shortened version of the "yes" template—on a daily basis whenever you experience stress, feel overwhelmed, or find yourself struggling. This practice of self-soothing can quiet the voices of the smaller parts of you, expand your sense of self, and bring into your present life the energy that has been stuck in the past.

4. When you've identified a part of you that's struggling alone with fear, ambivalence, or an overwhelming task or emotion, ask yourself the following:

- Who is this part of me that simply needs to be heard? How old are you? Are you a 500-million-year-old survival mechanism or a memory from childhood?
- How much must I expand to hold your feelings of sadness, shame, anger, or fear?
- What do you need to receive from me? Safety? Acceptance? Leadership?
- What role will help me shift to the more compassionate voice of my Strongest Self? A protective role? A leadership role?

Awaken the Five Qualities of Your Strongest Self

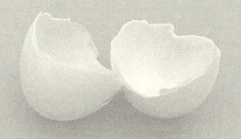

5

Safety Replaces Stress
Self in the Role of Protector

We should take care not to make the intellect our god; it has, of course,
powerful muscles, but no personality. It cannot lead; it can only serve.
—Albert Einstein

WHEN STEVEN FIRST CAME to my office his main complaint was
insomnia. But, in fact, his insomnia was brought on by a long-
term post-traumatic stress disorder and constant worry and vigilance. Only two other clients in the last twenty-five years
demonstrated as much fear, distrust of their environment, and
need for control as Steven, a very successful fifty-two-year-old
consultant and entrepreneur.

Steven was born just before the Blitz of London started in
1940. The sounds of sirens and the faces of worried parents and
nurses filled the early months of his life. Later the scars of the first
year of life would show themselves in the form of an inability to
trust that it was safe to go to sleep or to trust that adults could
protect him from harm. He learned to sleep with one eye open,
as if waiting for the sounds of sirens and bombs and the screams
of other children in the shelters and hospitals where he stayed.

For someone with Steven's experiences, the qualities of a Strong Self—especially safety, presence, and connection—are a basic necessity for recovery from early trauma, conditioned reactions, and attempts to cope by trying to control as much as you can. It took a little longer than a year of weekly therapy for Steven to show significant improvement in his symptoms. We used the steps outlined in this book, only we applied them more slowly in order to build trust in the ability of his subconscious mind to work for him while his conscious mind slept. A childlike part of him, frozen in the memories of the past, needed to know that a strong, adult self was there for him, to provide safety, presence, and connection.

Steven's recovery began with the seemingly simple step of first noticing the early signs of stress and vigilance. He followed up with a decision about the level of threat and then practiced consciously exhaling to float down into the support of a chair and the floor. These were steps he could take to prove to his mind and body that it was safe to let go of his breath, muscle tension, and the hypervigilance of his conscious mind. Repeated many times a day, this process showed Steven that he could begin to trust that the world—represented by the chair and the floor that literally held him—offered him a support system beyond the efforts of his conscious intellect and consciously controlled muscles.

The Stress Response Is Your Faithful Servant

We typically characterize stress in completely negative terms, but our body's reaction to stress—our *stress response*—is actually a healthy survival response. The stress response prepares us to cope with danger and threats to our well-being by stimulating the flow of dozens of hormones, primarily from the adrenal glands located over the kidneys. The sensitive mechanisms for survival are located in our earliest brains: the amygdala, located at the center of the mammal brain, sends messages to put our body on alert and triggers the fight-or-flight response of our reptile brain.

The usual physical symptoms of a stress reaction—sweaty palms, butterflies in the stomach, knees shaking, heart pounding —are signs that the stress response is doing its job of preparing us to fight or run. This protective survival reaction also speeds up the blood's clotting response and the body's immune system in case of injury or infection. Digestion is slowed or stopped; blood moves out of the stomach and extremities toward the heart and large muscles so we are prepared for fight or flight.

The emotion of fear and the body's stress response are normal, healthy responses that warn us of danger and threat. In animals these signals of danger are instantly turned into protective actions —running away and preparing to fight. In humans similar message-carrying chemicals prepare us to react but can be quieted in seconds once our most recently evolved brain sends a message back (and down to the lower brains) that the danger has passed and that we are safe, both physically and psychologically. Unlike animals, we have a brain that can interpret and regulate our lower brains' reactions. Too often, however, we interpret normal reactions as evidence that there's something wrong with us. But we can instead simply observe our conditioned reactions, make a decision, and choose how to act in ways that are appropriate for the situation and in accord with our overall strengths and values. It's these newly evolved executive-brain functions— observing reactions, regulating them, and choosing how to act— that distinguish us from other mammals and primates.

The healthy stress response only becomes a problem when our modern, evolved brain is not awakened to play its role in determining the appropriate level of threat and the appropriate human action. Without guidance, our primitive responses take over and can lead to chronic stress, as experienced in battle fatigue and job burnout. The damaging effects of chronic stress or distress— such as high blood pressure and adrenal fatigue—occur when we are kept in an environment of ongoing danger, or when we continue to believe that our worth and safety are threatened.

But we can learn to put our Strongest Self and the most developed part of our brain in a leadership role to determine when our physical well-being and sense of worth are safe. Our stress response will follow our lead and adjust accordingly.

One of the jobs of our new, human brain is updating the defaults set millions of years ago by our ancestral brains. The survival sensors of our lower brains are reactive to snakes, for example, but not to electricity or traffic. That's why you need to awaken your new brain so it can determine if the stress messages from its ancestral brains are accurate and appropriate for your life today. To unlock your full potential, you need to know these three things:

1. That you have a higher, Strongest Self and a new brain
2. How to awaken your Strongest Self
3. How to put your Strongest Self in charge of managing your life

After all, only you, from the perspective of your human brain, can see the real threats, challenges, and opportunities of today's world that brains formed hundreds of millions of years ago cannot comprehend.

The trick, of course, is to learn how to take on a protective role toward your body and life so you can soothe and calm yourself and your reptile brain instead of evoking a stress response by using self-threats and self-criticism. Then the process of generating messages of safety, compassion, and leadership that lower your stress hormones is relatively simple and rapid in most situations.

How to Manage Your Stress Response: Putting You in Charge of How You Feel

In order to put your Strongest Self in charge of how you react to stress, it's essential to understand that the stress response is evoked for three principal reasons:

1. To prepare you to cope with physical danger
2. To signal a psychological threat to your self-worth
3. To respond to your mind's images of threats from the past and images of work or danger anticipated in the future

Prepare for Physical Danger: Send a Message of Safety

Ironically, the easiest of these responses to manage is our body's reaction to real threats to our life, such as an earthquake, a gunshot, a hurricane, or a car accident. For example, if we were in good health, and an earthquake or a hurricane were to take place now, we would all experience the symptoms of a stress response. The reptile brain's fight-or-flight response would signal the adrenal glands to start pumping corticosteroids into our muscles to prepare us for danger. But if the earthquake or hurricane were to suddenly slow down, our human prefrontal cortex—the newest brain on the planet—would give the message "All is clear; we're safe."

By simply exhaling and thinking or saying, "This is only a 3.0 level earthquake on the Richter scale; we're safe" (or "That sound of a gunshot was only a truck backfiring" or "That snake is really a stick"), we communicate a message of safety. Remarkably, our oldest brain—the reptile brain—and the amygdala cooperate and shut off the stress hormones within thirty seconds. This is perfect mind-brain-body communication. It's one of the most empowering things you can do for yourself and one of the fastest ways to shift into your proper role as your Strongest Self.

A client named Barbara expressed the power of this shift very eloquently when she said, "The scared part of me is no longer my whole identity. . . . My Strongest Self has become a guardian toward that scared part. It's been so helpful to finally see the difference and to unburden my ego that gets so easily overwhelmed and stressed."

When you manage your life from your Strongest Self, you're empowered to gain the cooperation of the primitive brain's fight-

or-flight response. From your higher perspective—activated in the prefrontal cortex in your forehead—you make executive-brain decisions about the level of danger, the appropriate action to take, and when it's safe to relax. Fortunately, you don't need to learn how to give this signal of safety; you simply exhale and give a sigh of relief, which instantly signals the body's relaxation response—from the parasympathetic branch of the autonomic nervous system—to take over and release muscle tension and reduce stress hormones.

Post-traumatic stress disorder (PTSD), which involves the holding of traumatic, emotionally charged memories in the hippocampus and amygdala, requires serious therapy such as that provided by eye-movement desensitization and reprocessing (EMDR) to "metabolize" or break up deeply ingrained memories of trauma and severe stress. Consult with your doctor or therapist before applying the methods outlined in this book.

Cope with Psychological Threats: Send a Message of Worth and Connection

Earthquakes and hurricanes of a life-threatening magnitude don't happen every day or even every year, but threats to our worth and ego can happen several times a day. It is these mostly internal threats to our self-worth that are the cause of most of our stress.

When we limit our identity to merely that of a hardworking ego, separate from any support, we make ourselves vulnerable to threats of criticism, rejection, and loss of worth. We feel alone and believe we must struggle to protect ourselves with primitive methods of coping, such as perfectionism, addictive habits, and procrastination. We then try to avoid being vulnerable to rejection and criticism by either putting in extra time to make things perfect (perfectionism and workaholism) or by refusing to even try (procrastination and indecision). Worrying, self-criticism, and self-threats of misery and punishment are usually attempts to ensure that we'll obey the rules and, hopefully, avoid the criticism, judgment, and rejection of those who could punish us with separation from the love and approval we crave.

But threats—while temporarily effective in stopping risky behavior—can cause extreme stress and depression because they provoke a mammal-brain fear of abandonment that causes us to seek approval, physical warmth, and nurturing in order to survive. Adults who suffer rejection and infants who are abandoned seem to go through similar phases of physical and emotional hurt, crying, self-blame, and a willingness to comply in the hope of regaining acceptance and love. It's likely that this dramatic response to threats of abandonment is a primal attempt at physical survival that is not relieved by rational, left-hemisphere thought alone. We need to have an emotional connection with something beyond our ego identity, conscious mind, and emotional brain to heal such a basic fear of separation.

To lessen this form of stress, we can learn how to shift our identity from the worrier-critic to the self who can replace the critic voice with a voice of safety, compassion, acceptance, and connection. We can learn to move, as Robert Bly might say, from being the wounded child to being the one who has a child to protect and guide. It's as if a loving parent or a protective guardian angel arrives to comfort a frightened child with the message, "You are not alone. I accept you completely. I will never abandon you. I am always here for you. You will always have a home here."

Respond to Images of the Past or Future: Send a Message of Presence

Regrets and guilt about the past are often expressed in admonishments such as "You should have" or "You shouldn't have." Worry about anticipated danger in the future is expressed by the question "What if?" Each of these images of virtual realities evokes energy from your body that cannot be used now in the real world.

Calling up the stress response to deal with dangers that are not happening now is similar to pulling a fire alarm for a fire that happened twenty years ago or to fearing a fire that may happen next year. It would be unfair to the fire department and a misuse of its time and energy to ask firefighters to respond to such an alarm, just as it's unfair to demand that your body continually respond to threats of danger from events that cannot be tackled now. As I say in my seminars, anxiety is energy that cannot be used now. When you focus that trapped energy on action in the present moment, you release it and experience excitement and effectiveness.

Exercise: Create a Psychological Safety Net to Stop Unnecessary Stress

This exercise will give you a physical sense of how providing a psychological safety net for yourself will shift you from fear, stress, perfectionism, and procrastination to the safety necessary to perform optimally. Read this exercise and imagine or visualize—with your eyes opened or closed—what it feels like to be in each scene. Then notice how your mind and body respond.

Scene 1. Imagine that your job is to walk a board that is one foot wide, thirty feet long, and four inches thick, and that you have all of the ability necessary to complete this task. Can you take the first step without fear or hesitation? Let's assume that you say yes.

Scene 2. Imagine that your job is the same and that your ability is the same, only now the board is one hundred feet above the ground, suspended between two buildings. Can you do the task now? If not, what's stopping you? How much stress do you feel?

Where in your body do you feel tension (that is, reactions to signals of danger and stress)?

Most people answer that they're afraid of falling or making a mistake that could cause serious injury and probably death. This is an understandable and normal reaction.

Scene 3. While you've been stuck on this board, paralyzed by fear and hesitating to start or complete this task, your boss, friends, and family—who all know you can do it—are accusing you of procrastination and advising you to just do it. But you know it's not that easy. With so much at stake, you feel you have to do it perfectly—there's no room for mistakes—or else you'll die or feel like you're dying.

Suddenly, everything changes. You can feel heat behind you and can hear the crackling sounds of fire. The building supporting your end of the board is on fire! How will you overcome your hesitation and paralysis now? How important is it now to do the job perfectly? Are you still worried about falling? Do you tell yourself, "I work best under pressure and deadlines"? How do you break free of fear of failure and get yourself across the board?

Most of my clients and workshop participants answer that dignity and perfectionism are no longer a concern. They say they'd crawl, scoot along on their bottom, and scream if necessary to get away from those flames. Regardless of how you manage to get across that board to complete the task, notice how you shift from being paralyzed by fear to being motivated to do anything to survive.

Scene 4. In this final scene, imagine that the task and your ability remain the same, there's no fire or deadline, but now, four feet below the board, there's a strong net. Can you walk the board now? If so, what has changed for you? Note that you can still make a mistake, fall, feel embarrassed, or not do it perfectly.

Notice and write down the words and feelings that come with having a safety net under your board. You might say, "I won't die," "It won't be the end of the world if I make a mistake," or "I'm still afraid of heights, but knowing there's a safety net allows me to think about just doing the job instead of worrying about falling."

It might seem hard to believe, but giving yourself a psychological safety net will diminish most of what stresses you in life. However you choose to say it, make this message of safety the psychological and emotional safety net you give to yourself, every day. Write down and keep handy your personal message of safety, worth, and presence.

Put Your Strongest Self in Charge of Your Stress Response

As soon as you become aware of anxiety and stress, shift to the perspective and roles of your Strongest Self and—from the voice of the self—give yourself messages of safety, worth, and presence.

By practicing the shift from messages of stress to messages of safety you'll find that you're able to calm your body and focus your mind in less than a minute after a stressful thought or event. You'll have awakened your Strongest Self to take charge of your lower brain stress response, and it will respond to your voice and cooperate with your messages.

How to Manage Your Stress Response		
When Overreacting to . . .		**Do This**
physical danger	→	send a message of safety and acceptance
psychological threats	→	send a message of worth and connection
past or future images	→	send a message of presence and focus

Voice of the self. "Yes, I see your fears, and they are valid and normal. You no longer have to cope with them alone. I didn't mean to threaten you. Your Strongest Self is here and knows how to be in this world in a more robust, easy, and joyful way. Regardless of what happens or what others say, I'm always on your side. No matter what happens, we can get through it together. I will never abandon you. You're safe with me."

Result. Fear and panic are contained within a larger, safer home where there's support and protection. Self-threats are minimized or soon eliminated. The stress response follows the self's leadership and its decisions regarding the proper level of stress reaction. In your role as the protective self, you learn how to protect your sense of worth from judgment and begin to feel more self-reliant and secure and, therefore, less vulnerable to external pressures or internal threats.

Exercise for Chapter 5: Rate Your Stress Level

For one week rate your stress level on a scale of zero to ten. Zero represents those times when you felt the safest, and ten represents the times when you felt the most stressed.

Note: You can't have a ten every day. When you calculate the level of danger, decide if it is close to a ten (a message of extreme danger requiring high levels of adrenaline) or if it is closer to a three (a message of mild disruption). If your earthquake is in this lower number range, exhale and think or say, "It's only a three; we're safe. This is *not* the end of the world for us. Your worth is safe with me," or "I will not let this ruin our weekend or our evening."

Grade your stress level on a scale of zero to ten.

SAFEST   MOST STRESSED

| 0 | 1 | 2 | 3 | 4 | 5 | 6 | 7 | 8 | 9 | 10 |

By gauging your level of stress every day for one week, you'll discover that not every stressful event has to be an end-of-the-world disaster. You'll be amazed to discover that your body and lower brains will follow your message of safety, will quickly lower your heart rate and stress hormones, and will allow you to be effective and productive in less than a minute.

6

Choice Replaces Inner Conflict

Self in the Role of Negotiator

[There's a] universal quest for a lost sense of paradise that expresses itself in creation myths across cultures. It is not until mature individuals see that they are the creator of their own Self that the search for an external paradise gives way to self-soothing and internal sense of bliss.

—Joseph Campbell, *The Power of Myth*

A FEW YEARS AGO I was feeling upset because I needed to have a root canal. For days I repeatedly told myself, "You *have to* get a root canal." This message was telling my mind and body, "You have no choice. This is going to be painful. I'm going to force you to do something you don't want to do."

The pressure from this authoritarian voice provoked another part of me that naturally responded with, "I don't want to have to get a root canal." This rebellious part didn't want to accept the reality and consequences of tooth decay, nor did it want to be pushed around by a bully. This inner conflict between these two voices lowered my energy and made me feel like a depressed victim who could not accept responsibility for how much candy he had eaten or how infrequently he had flossed his teeth. Stuck in the inner conflict between these two voices and their narrow view of reality, I was procrastinating while my condition worsened and my pain increased.

Finally, with much ambivalence, I got myself to make an appointment with an oral surgeon. After examining my x-rays he told me, "I have bad news. I don't think we can do the root canal. You may have to lose the tooth. But let me take another x-ray to make sure." Ten minutes later he returned with the new x-ray and said, "Good news. We *can* do the root canal!" At which point I shouted back with genuine enthusiasm, "Great! Let's *do* the root canal."

I couldn't believe what I was hearing myself say. A few moments earlier I had felt ambivalent and depressed that I had to face dental surgery. In just a few minutes my entire mood had changed back to that of my true self, or Strongest Self. Simply seeing my real choices freed me of the conflict between the voices of "you have to" and "I don't want to." In that moment I discovered that seeing my choices helped me rapidly shift out of a passive, depressive mood. I also discovered that telling myself "you have to" makes me feel like a victim and just doesn't make sense if I'm still actually going to get the root canal or pay the taxes or the parking ticket and so on. I might as well face the unpleasant task without giving myself messages that cause inner conflict and get it over with as quickly as I can.

Inner conflict seems to be a normal consequence of our evolutionary and developmental history that gave us several brains with often-competing functions as well as a brain that is split into two hemispheres. By learning to act from the newest part of your brain—the only part that has the ability to choose—you break through inner conflict by asserting your Strongest Self's vision to unite all parts of you in a common effort.

Your Human Brain's Unique Ability to Choose

Conflict among our multilevel brains makes it difficult, and sometimes impossible, for us to choose among multiple needs, options, and warnings. To break the deadlock between conflicting parts—and overcome the chronic ambivalence, indecisiveness, and procrastination that usually result from inner conflict—we need to awaken the leader-negotiator part of our brain.

Sigmund Freud characterized inner conflict as a battle between the *superego* and the *id*. The part of us that speaks in the authoritarian, superego voice of "you should" and "you have to" is formed by the age of six and is concerned about following the rules in order to avoid punishment, shame, and abandonment. This function most likely stems from the socialization process that is part of every mammal brain. The pack, herd, or tribe imposes a hierarchical order that is supported by taboos and genetic wiring that makes possible a protective surrender-yielding response. This submission response, triggered by ancient biochemical mechanisms, stops aggressive action, allows society to maintain its hierarchical structure and parents to take charge of their young, and keeps us from fighting when the odds of winning are negligible.

By the age of six most children learn a self-scolding, or inner critic, voice in order to help them avoid parental and societal disapproval. They direct this superego voice primarily toward their own id, a spirited two-year-old voice that asserts its need for unconditional love and responds with, "But I don't want to" and "I want what I want when I want it." This part of us does not consider the caloric content of treats when we are attempting to diet, nor does it trim back its urge to shop when we are trying to keep a budget.

As Infants: Living with Unconditional Love

When we were infants, everything we needed was lovingly provided for us. Our simplest attempts at mimicking a sound or taking a step could make our mothers smile and our fathers applaud. We may have been helpless and dependent, but we were remarkably powerful in stirring love and joy in all those around us. For a time it was as if we were in our own garden of unconditional love.

When we reached the toddler stage, we wondered what ever happened to that blissful, easy time. How did we lose the power to receive unconditional love? By the time we started to walk into the world on our own two feet, unconditional acceptance usually had ended and paradise was lost. Love, or at least acceptance, became conditional as loving parents turned into authority figures who must warn us of dangers in *their* world and busy mothers were no longer available to watch over and support our every step. We couldn't possibly understand why we lost unconditional acceptance from our idealized parents, so we blamed ourselves. We asked, "Why did things change? What did I do wrong? Was I too demanding; too much for my parents to handle; too jealous when a baby brother or sister arrived?" The child's plea for a return of unconditional acceptance can haunt us into our adult life, kept alive by mammal-brain fears of abandonment and the belief that we did something wrong—or even worse, the belief that there's something fundamentally wrong with us.

Regardless of how or when it happens, we all experience the loss of unconditional acceptance that was so freely given during the first months of life when almost everything was easy. We will stay stuck in our search for an idealized past with perfect parents until our mature self shows up in a leadership role to direct our energies toward our present-day goals and to provide an internal sense of acceptance and peace.

The Toddler's World: A Life of Endless Adventure?

Toddlers rush into their world expecting to find a puppy or grandma behind every tree. They have a spirited love affair with their world and are not interested in the older generation's worries about traffic, mean dogs, chicken pox, or the stock market. They don't want anyone raining on their fresh experience of *their* world.

The brain of a toddler is still growing, and the hemispheres of the brain are still plastic—not yet divided into left-brain functions of language, detail, and linear thought as opposed to right-brain functions of nonverbal representations, holistic images, and spatial relations. The toddler's left-brain sense of self or ego is not yet separated from an oceanic bond with the universe through the right brain's subconscious genius. Children skip easily across brain hemispheres to effortlessly perform tasks—such as speaking in two or more languages—that, just a few years later, will take considerable struggle and work. Their still-integrated brain hemispheres give them a sense of magic about their world, and so life is an adventure of endless surprises and new abilities.

Ask any child of three or four how he or she drew a wonderfully colorful picture or constructed an entire drama out of toys and blocks and the child will tell you, "I don't know." With a shrug that is universal, a child at this age will tell you, "I don't know. It just comes to me. It's easy." As if to say, "Isn't all work easy, fun, and creative?" It's so easy when your ego's still in touch with its inner genius and isn't required to struggle alone to know everything. Don't you have an inner genius that makes things easy and fun to do?

The adventure of the two-year-old running fearlessly into his or her world is quickly ended when parents and society begin to impose limits and warnings with an endless series of "noes." And the child responds in kind. The repeated "no" of the child in the terrible twos expresses a desire for things as they once were—easy, loving, and accepting. The child's message of "no" can mean:

- *No*, I don't have to do anything to deserve your love. I am lovable just the way I am.

- *No*, I don't want to grow up and obey the rules of a world beyond paradise. My reality is more fun than yours.
- *No*, you're not the boss of me.

The Six-Year-Old's World: The Beginning of Inner Conflict and Rules

As children approach the age of six, they begin to understand that there has been considerable loss of power resulting from an unknown transgression and that obedience to the commandments and rules of society is necessary in order to maintain some form of acceptance and support. Having experienced, just a few years earlier, the loss of unconditional acceptance and threats of abandonment, they turn to learning the rules as an almost magical, superstitious way of holding on to a bit of the paradise and power they once had. Thus begins our inner conflict: a less adventurous, vigilant six-year-old fighting to avoid criticism, shame, and abandonment by trying to control the spirited and willful two-year-old part that tenaciously holds on to memories of unconditional love.

For the six-year-old child in us, a second fall from paradise, love, and blissful connection with others would be devastating. So we begrudgingly acknowledge that acceptance is now conditional and that we need to know the rules and commandments if we are to avoid punishment and abandonment.

For Avi, his former school was a place of comfort where he was considered an ideal child. He had many friends and knew how to get along with others and share toys. In his new school Avi was getting into fights and arguments with other boys, resulting in consequences and reports back home to his parents. He expressed upset and frustration to his mother: "But Mommy, at the other school we had a peace table where we could straighten things out, and the kids decided on the consequences. But we don't have that here. I don't know the rules in this new school. Mommy, I don't know the rules."

Avi's plea is typical of the six-year-old's transition away from paradise into a social world of laws, differences, punishments, and threats of isolation.

The Arrival of Choice: A Third Perspective

When a tug-of-war for our energy ensues between the voices of our six-year-old and two-year-old selves, we—the ones who must face adult projects, bills, and responsibilities in the real world of today—lose momentum and motivation. If we take the perspective of the six-year-old, we feel a sense of duty to parents, the law, and what's rational and right. If we overidentify with this part of us, we can become argumentative, dictatorial, and threatening toward others and the two-year-old part of us that wants unconditional love without being told, "But you have to obey."

When we're stuck in the two-year-old part of us, we want what we want and we can't make ourselves do what we don't want to do. If we identify too closely with our two-year-old ego, we feel resistant toward authority figures, tend to exhibit an uncontrollable temper, and are easily overwhelmed by tasks we don't know how to do immediately. To move toward our current goals, we must utilize a process that quickly recognizes when our energies are divided by inner conflict. To unleash the power of our true potential, we must learn to shift to a third perspective of adult leadership—replacing the inner conflict between the voices of "you have to" and "I don't want to" with the ability of our Strongest Self to operate from a fully evolved brain that permits us to assert "I choose."

Somewhere in our recent history—some say as little as five thousand to ten thousand years ago—a fully evolved *Homo sapiens sapiens* was able to deflect primitive fears and wants as well as internal voices that demanded, "You have to," in order to think or say, "I choose." If that moment were recorded on film, it would be accompanied by thunderclaps and a full symphony orchestra signifying that an earth-shattering event had just occurred—an event even more significant than when *Homo erectus*, almost two million years ago, overcame his mammal-brain fear of fire and harnessed it for survival.

Whether it happened twenty thousand years ago—in the caves of Lascaux, France, when an ancestor chose to paint a bison or perhaps an antelope or his or her own hand on the wall—or only five thousand years ago, someone made the first choice that required the awakening of higher consciousness in the human brain.

Integrating Your Actions with Your Goals, Values, and Commitments

After years of searching for the most effective way for my clients to learn how to achieve their goals, I've concluded that it's necessary to respect the survival intentions of our various parts and to gain their cooperation. Our ancestral brains were hardwired for survival in a world with challenges very different from those we face today. Our childhood methods of fulfilling our need for both dependence and independence may have been all that were available to us at that time. But our former ways of coping are ineffective and inappropriate for our current, adult skills, knowledge, and goals. From our awakened Strongest Self we need to update and guide our preset actions toward the achievement of our current goals. But who's in charge of your life today? Have you delegated control of your behavior and life to a two-year-old and a six-year-old who are in continual conflict?

Assume that your goal is to stop smoking or to lose twenty pounds. If after a month of much effort and some success, a part of you feels stressed or upset and wants to smoke a cigarette or eat an entire box of chocolates, how much control over these impulses would you have?

If you identify solely with the two-year-old part of you that wants what it wants regardless of the consequences, I can guarantee that you'll find yourself grabbing for the cigarette or the chocolates. You might justify your actions by saying, "It was a very stressful week and I wanted a cigarette. So I bummed a smoke, and then I bought a carton." In the instant that you became aware of a want, you reacted without thinking about your higher goals and your commitments to your body, your life, and your family.

I call this the two-step dance of life.

Step 1. You feel a need or a pain.
Step 2. You react by grabbing for a drug or an external fix.

This is a life that is run by your more primitive, automatic reactions. In the two-step dance, you are not in charge of the direction of your life, and uncooperative impulses easily sabotage your goals and commitments. You are reduced to behaving like a child who grabs what he or she wants without thought about the consequences and avoids what he or she doesn't want to face.

The more powerful, enlightened dance is a three-step.

Step 1. You feel a need or a pain.
Step 2. You—acting from the new and truly human brain—make a *choice* that is congruent with your commitments and values.
Step 3. You take action that is congruent with the choices and the leadership vision set by your higher self.

In the three-step dance, you have integrity. Your actions are integrated and are congruent with your values, goals, and commitments. You feel confident in your ability to gain the cooperation of every part of you in achieving your goals. Even when you face hard decisions, you have control over your wants and have tos and can choose to do what's in accord with the path you've chosen and committed to. In the three-step dance, you become a mensch —an evolved, wise person who's in charge of his or her life. Remarkably, the two- and six-year-olds cooperate with and support your leadership.

Claire: Breaking Free from Conflict

As an example of how to apply these concepts, consider the ambivalence and inner conflict experienced by Claire, a formerly healthy sixteen-year-old who now had to cope with diabetes. Claire found it extremely difficult to accept that her world had changed, that her body and life were no longer perfect. Taking insulin became a painful, daily reminder that life outside of paradise can be filled with have tos.

Claire's parents and doctor played the role of the authoritarian voice and told Claire that she was risking blindness, amputations, and kidney damage if she didn't comply with medical orders, take her insulin shots, and stop her reckless behavior. Like overly zealous and authoritarian six-year-olds, her parents thought they were being rational and realistic in trying to control a resistant, unrealistic two-year-old who would not take her medicine. In fact, they only contributed to the powerful inner conflict that kept Claire stuck in the role of a rebellious and resistant two-year-old. When their threats and pressure failed to gain Claire's compliance, they sent her to my office and gave me the instruction to "hypnotize her to take her insulin and to stop eating sweets."

Through trial and error, I had learned never to get into a tug-of-war with a two-year-old. Instead, I conscientiously avoided an authority figure's use of "you have to" and "no, you can't." I wanted to demonstrate for Claire the voice and role of a respectful self who could hear all of her fears and problems without argument. I, therefore, concentrated on offering her a lengthy application of the "yes" template.

Every time Claire told me that she didn't want to take insulin and wanted to eat candy, I responded with, "Yes" and "Yes, of course. That's perfectly normal and understandable." When she escalated her resistance and told me about going to a party, where she had cake, candy, and soft drinks, I simply said, "Yes, of course. That's just what a normal teenager would do."

After about thirty minutes with no arguments or pressure from me, Claire realized that she could relax her extreme opposition and move beyond the two-year-old's desperate attempt to hold on to the perfect world of infancy. At that point I asked her a question that implied she was ready to change her perspective by shifting to the role of a protective, adult self. I said, "If you had a little girl and she said she wanted to eat poison, would you let her eat poison?"

Claire responded, "No."

I continued, "But what if that little girl insisted and said, 'But it's sweet and I really want it.' Would you let her eat the poison?"

Claire answered, "No, of course not."

"Well," I said, "I'm so sorry to tell you that, for your body, too much sugar *is* like poison. And your body is like your little girl who needs your protection from eating poison and too many sweets. Will *you* protect her from poison and choose how much insulin to take when *you choose* to sample a little bit of sugar once in a while?"

Claire's face changed from that of a petulant child to that of a young woman with a serious responsibility, as she replied with an emphatic "Yes."

Shifting to the Role of Negotiator

When she was stuck in the two-year-old version of herself, Claire couldn't accept a world in which she was vulnerable to diabetes and must avoid sugar and take insulin injections. But in less than one hour, Claire shifted out of the frightened and rebellious position she was forced to take in opposition to the authoritarian voices and began to assume the role of a protective, mature self that can make difficult choices.

In a few more meetings, Claire learned to speak in the voice of her mature self that could accept the two-year-old's wants without being controlled by them. It also helped that her parents agreed not to act out the authoritarian roles they had been playing.

From her Strongest Self in the role of negotiator, Claire also could address the legitimate concerns of her six-year-old and relieve it of responsibility for her actions by offering a more effective and compassionate leadership voice and a negotiated solution.

Once the third perspective of her higher self was awakened in the roles of a protector and negotiator, a more mature Claire could mourn the loss of paradise, face her vulnerability to illness, and take the necessary steps to maintain her health.

From Claire's example we learn how rapidly this process works when we move into the role of a mature self who breaks through inner conflict by finding a middle ground of choice that's consistent with our current challenges, needs, and goals. To facilitate the process of gaining the cooperation of every part of us, we learn to switch to a higher perspective—a third place from which we can negotiate between the voices of "I don't want to" and "you have to." In this role of negotiator, we can exercise our ability to make choices with the knowledge our action and inaction have real consequences and rewards in the real world of real human beings.

Exercise for Chapter 6: Acting from Choice

1. Notice and listen for the words and feelings that accompany strong wants, resistance, and dictatorial shoulds. Consider most of these reactions to be messages from primitive aspects of yourself that require your Strongest Self to make an executive choice or decision. Notice which thoughts and feelings precede ambivalence, resistance, indecision, and procrastination.

2. Notice if you first hear the authoritarian "you should" voice of the six-year-old or the rebellious "I don't want to" voice of the two-year-old. This will let you know which side of the inner conflict you identify with most. Remember that even when you're aware of only one voice, the opposing voice is still there, holding on to the other end of that tug-of-war rope. You must address both sides.

3. Observe the tug-of-war between voices, parts, and wants, and provide a leadership direction and choice that is consistent with your adult objectives. You're using your human brain whenever you make a *choice*. Remember, you don't have to want to do the activity you're choosing. Choice is a third place that is neither "want to" or "have to." It only functions in a very different and new part of your brain.

4. Give yourself what you *need*, to paraphrase Mick Jagger, not necessarily what you *want*. By providing all parts of you with a leadership presence in the real world, you are hearing archaic reactions and connecting them to a flexible brain that can adapt to what's needed now. You don't always get what you want, but when you're heard, validated, and connected to a larger, stronger self, you'll get what you need. This, you will find, is more deeply satisfying than your wants.

5. Notice how leading from your Strongest Self, and its ability to choose, quickly frees you to follow through on achieving your goals without resistance or self-sabotage.

You can expect a feeling of empowerment as you break through inner conflict and gain the cooperation of all parts of you in moving forward on the path that you have chosen.

7

Presence Replaces Feeling Overwhelmed
Self in the Role of Leader

We need to change the way we measure time and to relax our insistence on control. . . . Instead of focusing on time running out, it should be a daily exercise . . . to mark the moment. The present never ages. . . . If every day is an awakening, you will never grow old. You will just keep growing.

—Gail Sheehy, *New Passages*

IN TODAY'S WORLD of multitasking to achieve multiple goals and of multiple distractions taking us off in another direction away from those goals, it's no wonder we often feel overwhelmed. Whenever we start a large project or attempt to tackle several tasks at once, our energy level rises from relative calm to overwhelming anxiety in just seconds. Anxiety (which I define as "energy that cannot be used now") can turn into panic if we add to our to-do list additional problems from the past and those anticipated in the future.

We feel overwhelmed when our time-traveling mind attempts to be in several places and times at once while our body remains in the reality of the present. The marvelous ability of the frontal lobes of our brain to imagine a virtual reality of activities that do not exist in the present is both an advantage and a potential problem. When used correctly, our frontal lobes offer us the ability to learn from past mistakes and to mentally rehearse, and prepare for, what we might need to do in the future to achieve our goals and avoid danger. If we fail to guide our mind back into the present where our body is, we will experience anxiety and feel overwhelmed.

Before there was a forehead with frontal lobes on this planet, prehuman creatures couldn't regret the past or worry about the future. They must have lived like people who've had a complete lobotomy—the surgical, chemical, or accidental removal of the frontal lobes. They would have been able to focus their attention and energy on what was required for their survival in the moment. While they could react to memories of past injuries, they really couldn't worry about them or feel overwhelmed about future threats. While at times we might envy their worry-free life and consider using surgery, alcohol, or drugs to diminish the time-traveling ability of our frontal lobes, we can learn how to center our mind in the present moment.

Feeling Overwhelmed by Multiple Goals, Demands, and Emotions

It's normal to experience a rush of energy at the start of any large project or challenging event or when we create images of multiple tasks in multiple time frames. It's also normal to be overwhelmed by conflicting emotions, such as attraction and fear of getting hurt. Feeling overwhelmed puts us into a frozen, deer-in-the-headlights posture that keeps us looking up at a mountain of work with no clear idea of where to start. It's as if we're trying to get to the top of that mountain or the end of a four-hundred-hour project in one exhausting leap, without focusing on the trailhead or on when and where to start. At such moments we often give voice to the conflicted messages we're giving ourselves: "I have to finish this enormous project. I've got so much to do, but I don't know where to start."

The ineffective leadership command "You have to finish a whole mountain load of work and do it perfectly" doesn't tell the workers where or when to start or on what work to focus their attention. The fact is that the moment of finishing will exist in the indefinite and imagined future, a virtual reality that your body can't get to. That leaves you stuck with more energy than you can use now and without a clear direction and time in which to release that energy.

We sometimes forget that our bodies evolved in a world of forests and savannahs before cell phones, beepers, traffic, or the ability of the human brain to create virtual realities of the past and future. To make productive use of our pent-up energy, our bodies need a leader to make a decision about what action to take in the real time of this moment. If your body could respond to ineffective leadership commands, it might say, "Your fear of failure and your images of multiple tasks have evoked enough nervous, overwhelming energy for running a one-hundred-meter race. But then you insist that I have to get to the end of a twenty-six-mile race or the top of the mountain. Which is it? Tell me where to focus all this energy you just called for. Tell me when to start."

Why Attempts to Cope with Feeling Overwhelmed Can Fail

If we spend more than a few minutes feeling anxious, with an overwhelming level of energy, we usually attempt to quiet our agitation by trying to escape through procrastination and addictive habits. This often leads to eating sweets, smoking a cigarette, watching television, or surfing the Internet—anything to avoid facing an overwhelming task that could make us feel nervous, incompetent, and inadequate. Instead of directing our energy toward productive action, we're sending our bodies a message that says, "Eat this, smoke this, drink this, and shut up."

Another attempted solution for coping with overwhelming projects is to focus only on the details. Working from this nose-to-the-grindstone perspective may seem productive but actually is just busywork that occupies our minds and calms our energy and results in work that is not in line with our blueprint. If you don't consult the blueprint when building the foundation of your home, you're likely to waste a lot of energy and good cement.

Focusing only on the details can lead to workaholism—constant work without regard to priorities or direction. For example, some writers I've worked with are constantly producing stacks of journals with stories that are not connected to a central concept. One writer has four drawers of a file cabinet filled with unrelated stories, but not one outline on which to string these stories into progressive chapters. She works hard but doesn't complete anything coherent because of her fear of facing the overwhelming specter of a three-hundred-page book and two thousand hours of work over the next two years. In addition, she is overwhelmed by her fear of being criticized and rejected. So she just keeps busy—thus avoiding self-criticism for not working—but can't get herself to start work on a viable plan that could be rejected by an agent or publisher.

Three Things You Can Do When You Feel Overwhelmed

A client named Jim, who was coping with the rapid expansion of his newly successful business, called me in a panic. He said, "I have so many medical and work problems that I can't seem to relax. I'm overwhelmed. I'm taking a dozen medications and I still can't sleep. I wake up at three in the morning, worried about my job, money, and my health. Tell me what to do."

I suggested that Jim do three things:

1. Center on the present and rein in his time-traveling mind by starting on one small step of one project for no more than thirty minutes.
2. Create a four-dimensional overview or blueprint of his tasks, spread out over space and time—similar to a project manager's flowchart.
3. Shift his perspective, role, and voice to that of a leader and project manager who can keep his mind aware of both the overview or blueprint and the details of each step of the project.

Number 1: Center in the Present

I could've recited to Jim any number of lines from New Age or Eastern philosophies, such as, "There is only now. Trying to hold on to what is impermanent will only add to your suffering." But I knew that telling him these things wouldn't do him as much good as having him perform a simple centering exercise to bring his mind into the present moment.

I asked him to focus on his breathing, paying particular attention to the physical sensations of relaxing deeper into the support of the chair with each exhalation. Within six breaths he found that he was calming down. Then I demonstrated for him how he could talk to himself whenever his conscious mind was trying to tackle so many problems, instead of focusing on one task or going to sleep. I suggested that he do this exercise for himself once an hour, before starting any work projects, and just before going to bed.

I told Jim that by breathing in three parts, he'd train his body to automatically shift from the stress-induced reactions of holding his breath and tensing his muscles to exhaling as a signal that it's safe to release the stress hormones and muscle tension. Then he'd experience the feeling of floating down into the support of the chair, which symbolizes his connection to the rest of his brain and the wisdom of his body. By using this exercise of centering in the present throughout his day, Jim found that feelings of support and connection began to replace worry and anxiety.

The Centering Exercise. Do this centering exercise for yourself. Sit in a chair with your feet on the floor, rest your hands on your lap or on your legs, and take three to twelve breaths in three parts, as follows:

1. Notice your breathing and inhale for a count of three.
2. Hold your breath for a count of three; tighten your fists and your leg muscles, and pull your navel to your spine.
3. Exhale slowly and completely for a count of four to six, releasing all muscle tension as you feel yourself float down into the support of the chair and the floor.

Read the following instructions and consider recording this exercise or having a friend read it aloud so you can close your eyes, concentrate on quieting your energy, and release muscle tension.

• As you exhale, feel yourself float down into the chair and the floor, which represent something more powerful than your mind or ego struggling alone. That something could be your Strongest Self, the support of the earth, the laws of the universe, the deeper wisdom of the integrated left and right hemispheres of your brain, or, if you wish, God or another higher power.

• As you bring your attention to your body and the sensation of floating down into the chair with each exhalation, feel the chair backing you up. Notice the warmth of the chair on your back. As you turn your attention to the sensations you're feeling in the present, you're communicating to your mind and body:

"It's safe to be here for the next few minutes. There's nothing much for you to do and no place to go. You can release that tension. You can let go of trying so hard. I am choosing to sit still, here, in this moment—the only there is."

• Say, "Yes, hello" to any thought or part of yourself that tries to hold on to the past or to control the future. Bring that part and your time-traveling mind into the present by saying, "Yes, I hear you. I'm here for you now. You don't need to solve past or future problems alone. Come and be with me in this moment."

• Reassert your commitment to protect your body and your life, and catch and hold all aspects of yourself with compassion and understanding. Empowered by your leadership role, guide all aspects of yourself to this moment of vacation from worries about the past and future. Focus your attention on what you can do now to optimize your chances of achieving success and inner peace.

• Take a moment to record in your notebook any physical and emotional changes you observe.

Summary: One Minute to Center in the Present. This summary of the centering exercise will train your mind to expect a transformative shift in energy and focus within just twelve breaths. (You'll find a complete version of the centering exercise in Appendix B.) Use this one-minute exercise at least five times a day to ease your transition to any new task or situation. You'll discover that within two weeks of applying this exercise, you'll be significantly calmer and more creative and productive in your work and relationships.

• In three breaths exhale away thoughts and images of work from the past as well as your old, limited sense of self and its stories and problems. Free your mind from images of work and problems from the past. Let go of the last telephone call. Free yourself from the frustrations of a meeting or a commute.

• In three breaths exhale away thoughts and images of work in the future. Free your mind from the imagined future.

• In three breaths let your mind and body know that you are choosing to float down into the present with this work or this person, in this moment. Rest your conscious mind in the present where it connects with your body and the wisdom of your subconscious, dreaming mind.

• Take three breaths to count up from one to three. Count one and say, "I'm curious and interested about how rapidly I'll go from not knowing to knowing." Count two and say, "I'm choosing to be here, shifting from worry to wonder." Count three and say, "I am connecting to a deeper wisdom and am alert and eager to begin." Then slowly open your eyes and focus on your task.

Number 2: Create an Overview

When faced with large projects or a number of projects, most of us will immediately go from feeling overwhelmed to getting overly absorbed in the details. This creates two levels of unproductive work. At both extremes—the overwhelmed, anxious level and the detailed, more comfortable level of energy—we tend to lose sight of our mission, purpose, and priorities.

If you imagine that your task is like climbing a mountain, then pressing your nose against the mountain—which gives you only a two-dimensional view of the job—and trying to jump to the top would cause you to feel overwhelmed. To feel even more overwhelmed and anxious, try to make all your decisions about the entire journey to the top while looking up from the bottom. This assumes that, instead of getting more information as you climb, you must know everything that will happen while still at the bottom of the mountain. Focusing only on the details is like climbing the mountain with your nose on the ground for fear of looking up and getting overwhelmed about the enormity of the job.

To avoid the counterproductive extremes of either being overwhelmed or being stuck in the details, develop a four-dimensional overview, blueprint, or outline that spreads the tasks over space and time. With a four-dimensional view—height, width, depth, and time—of how to climb the mountain, you can see the path up the mountain spread out over the next few hours or days. You have time to enjoy the views, have lunch, and make informed decisions about which trails to take as you climb, gain a better perspective, get smarter, and adjust to the altitude. With practice you'll learn that you can't know everything at the start of a climb or a project. You'll actually get smarter and more confident along the path to the top.

Using "Back-Timing" to Complete Large Tasks or Projects. Let's assume that most large projects and multiple tasks will initially evoke an anxious level of energy and make you feel overwhelmed. After your initial reaction, you have three main choices:

1. Escape and avoid by using procrastination and distractions to temporarily lower your tension.
2. Focus on the details without making an overview or a plan.
3. Create a four-dimensional overview that gives you an outline of the steps of the project.

This last option allows you to make an informed decision about which details to focus on for a limited period—say, no more than thirty to ninety minutes—before checking with your outline or blueprint to ensure you're doing the right work and going in the right direction. By keeping your initial commitments to short periods of time, you'll avoid the fear of ignoring the other projects that are demanding your attention, and you're less likely to make costly deviations from your blueprint.

The blueprint or overview serves as a midstation between overwhelming levels of energy and calm levels for detail work. It gives you time to consider the big picture and to calmly choose the next detail on which to focus and helps you develop the appropriate sequencing of your project. Now that your mind has a blueprint to consult, it can more appropriately use its frontal lobe capability of planning and imagining the future to guide you to success-assured steps. With each segment of detailed work connected to the blueprint, you can feel assured that the foundation of your home will be in line with your plans, priorities, and schedule. When you create a four-dimensional outline of your tasks, you'll see that an important job is not finished all at once but is built in small, discrete steps over time. To get to the future place of finishing, you must tell your mind and body where and when to start.

If you want to be on time at the airport for your flight, you know that you can't give your mind only the flight's departure time. You must create a *back-timing* schedule. So for you to catch a 6 P.M. flight, you should arrive at the airport by at least 5 P.M., which requires that you leave your office by 4 P.M. and complete some calls by 3:30 P.M. You'll also need to back-time to the night before your flight so you can get your luggage packed and your tickets ready. You keep back-timing along your four-dimensional schedule until you know what to do *now* that contributes to your timely arrival at the airport.

Use this example as a model for how to back-time on any project. Take a moment to think about a big project—painting the living room, losing ten pounds, learning to play an instrument, completing college—and set a reasonable deadline in weeks, months, or years from now. Write the date of the deadline on the top of a page. Then back-time from the deadline and, moving down the page, write in each week or month until you come to today. Then ask yourself, "When can I start today? On what part will I start?" After you've completed at least thirty minutes of uninterrupted work on the project ask yourself, "When can I start again?"

You've just created a mental image of a project that spreads out into the future, like steps toward your goal, but also returns your mind to the present where your body can release its energy and start working. By creating four-dimensional views of projects, you're not only overcoming feeling overwhelmed, you're using the full potential of your new, human brain.

Number 3: Shift to the Leadership Perspective, Role, and Voice of the Self

Regulating the time-traveling mind and using its evolved skill to our advantage is the challenging job of our human prefrontal cortex. Without the guidance of our Strongest Self's new, executive-brain functions, we tend to feel guilty about the past, worry about the future, and overwhelm ourselves with multiple demands in the present.

Just as our human brain can signal the reptile brain to turn off its stress response and the mammal brain to turn off its signals for shame and surrender, our human brain can bring our frontal lobe images of the past and future into the present where the body must be. Like most evolved functions, our ability to mentally time travel helped our ancestors to survive and, therefore, cannot be eliminated. But we can learn to use our higher brain functions to quiet and redirect these ancient survival functions by providing a leader that is committed to living in the reality of the present moment.

Your Strongest Self Can Accept Your Human Limits. In the role and perspective of a leader, you have commitments to your body and life that require you to be realistic about the limits of your time and resources. As the leader you must make the tough choices about which activities and projects to focus on and which ones to let go. Fully accepting yourself as human is a very loving act that mourns the loss of the infant's fantasy that he or she should be all-powerful and capable of making others happy. Accepting your human limits also stops the pressure to be perfect and commits you to acting in the present rather than trying to change the past or control the future.

From your leadership role you can activate the voice of your Strongest Self that speaks to the panicked parts of you and your lower brains and says:

- *Yes*, you are overwhelmed with all the things you would like to do and feel you have to do.
- *Yes, of course* you are worried about the future and feel guilty about the past.
- *Yes*, I know better than anyone how you feel when you're overwhelmed and panicked.
- *And now* I'm here. You're not alone. And *I'm choosing* what to let go of, what to focus on, and what to commit to.
- I'm strong enough to deal with the expectations and anger of others. I will commit our limited energy and time to those tasks that are consistent with our higher values and mission.
- All you really need to do is to show up in the present moment, focus on starting, and watch yourself go from not knowing to knowing. This is going to be interesting.
- I'm choosing to be more at peace with life and to savor what it provides in the present moment. I can let go of trying to fix the past and control the future. This moment and this task are the only things you need to focus on. This is the only moment we have, and I intend to savor it and make the most of it.

The limited perspective of your isolated, struggling ego causes this part of you to easily feel overwhelmed by multiple tasks and the demand to wear many hats at home and on the job. By connecting all parts of yourself to your Strongest Self, you gain access to your subconscious, dreaming mind's four-dimensional perspective, making it possible to see tasks spread out over time as in a flowchart, a blueprint, or an outline.

Shifting your perspective from your conscious mind's limited, all-at-once view of many tasks to your Strongest Self's overview allows you to quickly calm yourself with a plan that is laid out in manageable segments over time and space.

The Self Is Able to Contain More of Your Feelings

When I was in graduate school at the University of Maryland, my father died of a stroke. A year later, my beloved grandfather died, an uncle died in an accident, a childhood friend died of cancer, and my fiancée broke off our engagement. In addition to these losses, I was having a difficult time with one of my psychology professors. As I was leaving his class—once again frustrated by the friction caused by our different points of view—all of the separate losses of the prior two years overwhelmed me and a deep sadness and physical pain swept over me. The ache in my heart and stomach caused me to double over as I walked—head down, with tears in my eyes—across campus to my next class. The only thing I was aware of was a sharp pain that was both emotional and physical.

I was focused only on the details of my losses and was worried about my future. My emotions had created an overwhelming mountain of feelings that I couldn't handle all at once. I was thinking, "Can I finish graduate school? Will I ever find another girlfriend? How will I bear any more losses?" My vision and feelings were limited in that moment to a small part of who I was. I was oblivious to my surroundings and a larger sense of self until I heard an explosion—like the sound of a big firecracker—and looked up. Suddenly, I was awake to the sights and sounds of a college campus in the early 1970s. Dogs were running after Frisbees, long-haired students were flirting under two-hundred-year-old trees, and my own body was moving through green expansive lawns under a clear blue sky. This Technicolor world was in stark contrast to my dreary, grayish pain. There was a larger, vibrant world all around me. I now had a larger container for my feelings and thoughts.

As my awareness instantly expanded to include the backdrop of the campus, the pain lessened, or at least it became only one small part of a much larger experience of life. This sudden shift was remarkable and reminded me of an awareness exercise I had learned in a class on Fritz Perls's Gestalt therapy. Following the guidelines of the exercise, I began to observe how my mind's attention shifted, and I said to myself:

Now I'm aware of my legs walking. Now I'm aware of the pain in my stomach . . . of the sound of women laughing . . . of the blueness of the sky . . . of feelings of sadness . . . of appreciating the beauty of this campus . . . of the sadness still being here, but being smaller . . . of my muscles and the strength of my body. Now I'm aware of being able to hold the feelings of sadness in a larger container that makes them seem less overwhelming.

The "Now I'm Aware of . . ." Exercise. The "now I'm aware of . . ." exercise is another tool for guiding your mind back into the present. It demonstrates your ability to shift your attention from seemingly overwhelming feelings to a calm focus on the larger world of this moment. To train yourself to hold disturbing feelings and concerns in a larger container of awareness, perform this exercise outside while walking or hiking. Rather than allowing your initial thoughts and feelings to take control of your full attention, think of them as only a small part of your larger, Stronger Self. With practice you'll be able to expand your capacity to carry your emotions, thoughts, and reactions without losing yourself to feeling overwhelmed by them. Within weeks of doing this exercise every day, you'll be able to quickly break free of obsessive thoughts about losses and difficulties in your relationships, in your job, or with your health.

As you begin this exercise, take a moment to become aware of what you're feeling in your body. Become aware of what you're seeing, smelling, and hearing as well as of your thoughts, images, and emotions. Notice how the object of your attention will continually change. Use the phrase "Now I'm aware of" to begin each statement, as in the following examples:

- Now I'm aware of discomfort in my left shoulder.
- Now I'm aware of the sound of a bird chirping and the noise of the traffic.

- Now I'm aware of a feeling of anxiety.
- Now I'm aware of a feeling of sadness.
- Now I'm aware of the soles of my feet pressing into the earth . . . the movement of my legs . . . the smell of the air in my nostrils.
- Now I'm aware of having many feelings that keep changing.
- Now I'm aware of a smaller sense of sadness being held in this larger awareness.
- Now I'm aware of the white puffiness of the clouds.

When you make the "now I'm aware of . . ." exercise a regular part of your coping skills, you'll find that all your thoughts, physical sensations, and emotions can be held by your expanded identity in a larger container. This practice shifts you to the perspective of yourself as observer. Through the perspective of your Strongest Self, you connect your mind with your body in the present, your right-brain hemisphere with your left, and your higher, human consciousness with your subconscious mind.

Exercise for Chapter 7: One Rapid, Focused Breath

Imagine that you're playing the role of a hero in an adventure movie or a kung fu or karate movie. Picture yourself in a scene in which five to ten opponents attack you simultaneously. Or simply imagine a typical day in which your boss, children, friends, and parents are demanding your attention and time, all at once.

- Notice the feeling of being overwhelmed and indecisive about what to do.
- Notice that, for a split second, you are holding your breath and have the wide-eyed reaction of someone frozen in fear and dread—the deer-in-the-headlights look.

- Notice that exhaling rapidly, as if giving the traditional explosive grunt of a black belt in karate, instantly focuses your eyes and hands on a single opponent or task and then quickly shifts your attention to the next one.

When you're confronted with your bills, dozens of e-mails or phone messages, or the simultaneous demands of multiple children or supervisors, use the karate grunt or the shout of a rapid exhalation to focus your attention and hands on one task. Bring your mind into the present to start here, now: "Focus! Confront those bills. Attack those files." Or shout the word "Now!" to break free of feeling overwhelmed. Make it a habit to exhale forcefully as you focus your attention on one task. The imprinting of this habit will rapidly replace your feeling of being overwhelmed with a productive release of energy in the present moment.

8

Focus Replaces Self-Criticism
Self in the Role of Teacher

Life exists only at this very moment, and in this moment it is infinite and eternal. You may believe yourself out of harmony with life and its eternal Now; but you cannot be, for you are life and exist Now.
—Alan Watts, *Become What You Are*

ONE OF THE MOST EFFECTIVE and powerful applications of the Awaken Your Strongest Self program is in dealing with time-pressured, high-stress situations, such as projects with impending deadlines, daylong standardized exams, three-day professional licensing exams, competitive sporting events, musical performances, and presentations before large audiences. To perform optimally in such situations, you can't let your ego or conscious mind worry about how you should've prepared in the past, the consequences of future failure, or an analysis of what's wrong with you.

The athletes, musicians, students, court reporters, and lawyers I've worked with have learned to use this program to perform optimally under intense pressure and time limits. Their achievements serve as evidence that all of us can learn to catch our reactive habits within seconds so that we can guide ourselves toward an optimal performance in any field, under any kind of pressure. That means that when your worrying mind is saying, "What's wrong with me?" your Strongest Self can focus your attention on doing the task rather than wasting time in self-criticism. Before you can finish cursing over spilled milk, you'll be back in the game and focused on what you can do now to clean it up and get on with the really big stuff of life. As you commit to your vision of working from your higher self—with all parts of you acting as an integrated whole—it will become easier for you to stay focused on your higher values and on maximizing your chances of achieving your goals while maintaining a sense of inner peace.

Self-Criticism and the "Genius Syndrome"

When I was conducting Conquering Test Anxiety workshops for students at the University of California, Berkeley, I noticed that their most distracting and upsetting thoughts were about the future outcome of their exams and on inner dialogue that was self-judging and self-critical. Their typical inner dialogue was future oriented and included self-judgmental and self-critical statements such as these:

- I've got to get an A in order to get into a good school. What if I have to tell my parents I failed?
- I can't understand this stuff. What's wrong with me?
- I should've studied more. I'm no good at math.
- I'm always procrastinating until the last minute. I'll never graduate at this rate.

Thoughts about the past or the future cause anxiety and stress—scattered energy levels that cannot contribute to a focused, optimal performance—and distract our minds from what we can do now. Self-critical thoughts about personal short-comings distract us with the worry that there's something fundamentally wrong with us. This form of self-criticism is what I call the *genius syndrome*. When our ego is caught in this syndrome, we say to ourselves, "I'm supposed to know this stuff immediately. But I don't know it, so there must be something wrong with my mind. I won't accept my normal human limits and possible failure. I'd rather get angry with myself because I'm not perfect, not God, and not a genius for whom everything should be easy. If it's not easy I won't even try."

The Zone of Optimal Performance

Peak performance experts Drs. Charles Spielberger and Richard Suinn have researched what is required to operate in the zone— that state of calm concentration that allows us to perform far beyond our usual skill and confidence levels (or, as you may recall from Chapter 2, that place of extraordinary performance that far exceeds what's possible through conscious effort alone). They tell us that results on exams and in sports improve significantly when we learn to replace ego-oriented, self-critical distractions with a task-oriented focus. Their research with college students and the U.S. Olympic team supports the techniques presented here to help you work, play, and relate from a center of calm focus. Dr. Mihaly Csikszentmihalyi of the Claremont Graduate University has discovered that those who work and perform with grace, joy, and ease are in a similar state that he calls flow.

What *you* can achieve—in the zone—as a total, integrated Strongest Self cannot be grasped by your ego, your old identity, or your conscious mind. The confidence level of your ego is irrelevant to what you can do when you *choose* to show up with resources of your integrated brain and Strongest Self. The research on working in the zone or flow state shows that focused attention on the task at hand creates a state of blissful involvement and enhances performance to levels that far exceed those possible when your ego and conscious mind struggle alone. To achieve an optimal performance in any situation, you must also be aware of and prepared for your usual distractions—such as self-criticism and thoughts about the future—so you can instantly push them aside and replace them with focused attention on one task in the present moment.

Those who consistently perform in states of flow or the zone are aware of a little-known secret: even when you think you're losing, or when you lack confidence in your ability to achieve your goal, you can reach levels far beyond your expectations by entering the zone. If you're operating only from ego—using only your conscious mind and controllable muscles to solve problems—you're working too hard. Connect with the genius that occupies the other 95 percent of your brain, and you'll find that confronting life's challenges and succeeding can be easier, creative, and exciting.

Staying in the Zone

Some go to a monastery to meditate in order to attain a spiritual awakening. Most of us, however, can achieve similar levels of awareness by going about the ordinary tasks of our lives with greater focus, presence, and mindfulness, while acting from our higher self.

Ever since I read about Zen Buddhism and Taoism in the books of J. D. Salinger, D. T. Suzuki, and Alan Watts, I've been fascinated by the idea of learning Zen archery and making Zen foul shots—the essence of peak performance without performance anxiety. As a teenager I thought of athletes who play in the zone as monks who practice a Western form of meditation. In that slow-motion moment of shooting the perfect foul shot, you're in the doing of it, not striving for the future goal or to reach any particular place.

The paradox is that professional athletes must be very goal oriented and competitive, but to reach their optimal level of play, they also must be able to focus their minds in the present moment. Any thoughts about the future goal or the remaining seconds on the clock would pull them out of the zone and back into ordinary, conscious-mind struggles.

Bill Cole, M.A., author of *The Mental Game Coach Report*, says that "Tiger Woods does not keep his eye on the goal. Instead, he focuses on the process. It's a myth that, in a competition, great athletes focus on the goal of winning. . . . What excellent performers focus on is process. Tiger is superb at keeping his mind in the here and now."

As you practice going beyond your everyday identity to live from your Strongest Self, you increase your chances of attaining inner peace and optimizing your potential. Yet you're content to be in the moment, knowing that consistent performance at optimal levels does not come from the efforts of a grandiose and struggling ego. It's an almost spiritual practice, such as when a surfer becomes one with the wave, a lover risks opening his heart, or a skydiver leaps into the arms of Mother Nature and says, "I don't know how to do this without your help. Show me a surprise." Remarkably, if you are persistent in showing up to life, life answers, "Yes, I'm here for you. You don't have to know how to do this alone. Just show up focused in the present, and watch for the surprise."

Most of us experience this spirit of playfulness with life when on vacation. In the safety of a time separated from everyday worries, we allow ourselves to drop our to-do lists and have tos and say to ourselves, "I'm free of pressure for two weeks. Regardless of what happens, I'm going to have fun! I intend to enjoy myself." And we do enjoy being with ourselves in a variety of adventures in which we don't know the language, the currency, or the transportation system. We can't make a mistake because there are no shoulds about how to do it. Everything is a learning experience and a new world to explore, much the way the world is for a toddler. Once again we experience a childlike love affair with life and our ability to be fully and easily in the world.

How to Remain Focused on the Task

Remember that you don't have to wait for your ego to feel secure, confident, motivated, and all-knowing. The first step in breaking free of your ego's limited identity and expanding to become your Strongest Self is to simply observe and identify your initial reactions and inner dialogue. From the self's perspective and empowering roles you can perform optimally by focusing on the task rather than on your ego's fears and distractions.

To achieve a personal best performance, do the following:

• Notice if the language and feelings of your ego-oriented thinking are focused on the past or future and on self-criticism.
• Simply observe and identify the feelings (usually anxiety and depression) that accompany ego-oriented thoughts. This is not the time to argue with them or to let thoughts or feelings distract you from your focus on the task at hand.
• Shift your focus to your mission and objectives and to what you can do now. Reassert your ability to choose to face any fear and start any task.
• Replace your initial default reactions and thoughts with task-oriented thoughts and directives, such as, "Focus here. What part of this answer do I know? What can I do now? I'm determined to show them what I can do. I'm in this game all the way through to the last second, regardless of the score."

It is important that you don't waste time arguing with the insecure, self-critical part of you or reassuring it with "It's OK." Simply say, "Yes, I know your fears. Focus here now. I'm choosing to show up to see what we can do.

Identify Your Default Reactions: Do They Contribute to or Detract from Your Mission?

When I was undergoing nine months of weekly chemotherapy, the first thing I told myself was, "The cancer didn't simply spread to my lung; it's held there by my lung's ability to filter debris from the bloodstream. My body is an active ally, not a passive victim." I began to see that certain thoughts and actions clearly contributed to feeling alive in the moment and other thoughts distracted me from my mission of living as fully as I could for as long as I could. My life became very simple. When deciding what to do, I would ask myself repeatedly, "To be or not to be? Does this thought or action contribute to my health, well-being, and aliveness—or does it detract?"

Because my top priorities, mission, and role as protector of my time, body, and life were so very clear, it took me only seconds to decide how to act. With a laserlike focus, I would instantly let go of negative thoughts and focus on my mission, path, and higher values. In carrying out my commitment to myself, at times I'd respond to a request from my friends and family with, "No, thank you. That sounds like work." Telemarketers heard, "No, thank you. I don't have the time." And when you've been given a terminal diagnosis, you can say, "I don't have the time" with true conviction.

Clarity of mission makes it easier to stay on course and to minimize diversions that might too easily waste precious time and energy.

Define Your Mission: Focus on a Stronger Life Passion

As you apply this program to your life, you'll learn that you can reap its benefits even when the more cautious parts of you aren't convinced that it will work. Remember, self-doubt is your ego's default position. Push it aside and choose to show up and follow the steps that focus you on moving forward with your new and stronger life passion.

You can use task-oriented thinking to perform optimally on exams, on the playing field, in business, and in relationships. But more than that, staying task-oriented on everyday projects is a way to practice breaking free of your ego's fears, self-doubts, and addictions by staying in the role of your Strongest Self. It's a way of learning that you don't have to be controlled by old habits or distracting thoughts and feelings. For example, I still have thoughts about smoking a cigarette even though I stopped smoking thirty years ago. But thoughts and even cravings—regardless of how strong they may be—can't control how I choose to act when I have such a solid commitment to protect my body from tobacco, old habits, and addictions. Having put my body through chemotherapy and more than ten years of smoking before that, I simply can't betray it with a cigarette regardless of how powerful the impulse to smoke. Now I can observe the thought of smoking, and even the impulse to smoke, with great curiosity and compassion. Instead of compelling me to smoke, these thoughts and feelings are simply outdated reactions that remind my Strongest Self to keep its commitment to the mission of protecting my body and my life.

The more clearly you identify your default reactions to life challenges, the sooner you'll be able to catch them and redirect all parts of you to the path that leads to inner peace and success. Recognizing your old habits and maintaining a clear mission work in concert to increase the speed with which you can self-correct and refocus on productive actions that lead to an optimal performance.

By linking awareness of your default reactions to corrective action, you'll become incredibly efficient and effective at limiting the destructive effects of the five major problems areas of stress, inner conflict, feeling overwhelmed, self-criticism, and struggle. You'll be able to respond to these problems in just seconds, replacing them with the qualities of your Strongest Self.

Mission Statements. A good way to remain committed to your life's missions and stay in the role of your Strongest Self is to create mission statements. To help you create an overarching sense of mission, I've listed my mission statements and vision as examples. (Note that *I* means "my Strongest Self" in its leadership and protective roles.)

- *I* am committed to accepting reality rather than fighting against it. Life and other people are not a problem or enemies but are simply facts.
- *I* limit my stress reaction to less than thirty seconds. Self-threats are no longer acceptable. *I* communicate to every part of me, "Your worth is safe with me. Regardless of what happens, *I* will not make you feel bad."
- *I* manage my life from choice rather than the ambivalence that's caused by the inner conflict between "you have to" and "I don't want to." Ambivalence and inner conflict are now wake-up calls for my Strongest Self to make an executive choice.
- *I* rapidly move from an isolated, worrying conscious mind and shift it to wondering what the deeper wisdom of my larger, integrated mind and body will achieve.
- *I* take at least three deep breaths before starting to work in order to connect with a deeper system of support, to link my left brain with my right brain, and to connect with the wisdom of my body.
- *I* integrate every part of me into a powerful, focused team. No single part of me works alone or carries full responsibility for my life.
- *I*, as my Strongest Self—not the six-year-old or the two-year-old or any of my lower brain functions—am in charge of my life. From the perspective, wisdom, and support available to me as my larger self, *I* take responsibility for my life and the role of guiding all parts of me toward my higher values and mission.

In your notebook, write down your own mission statements and commitments to yourself. By clarifying your mission statements, you'll move rapidly to the role of a teacher who keeps every part of you focused on seeing your current task to completion.

Exercise for Chapter 8: Focused in One Breath

In this exercise you'll train yourself to become centered within yourself in the time it takes to complete one to three full breaths. Do this exercise every time you notice self-criticism, worry, or frustration. If you do this exercise several times a day, in one week you'll significantly shorten the time you spend distracted from your higher vision.

1. The next time you find yourself tightening your fists or your jaw, furrowing your brow, and starting to curse because something isn't going your way, see how quickly you can exhale and float down into your chair, the soles of your feet, and the earth or the floor. (*Note:* a good time to practice this is when you're stuck in traffic.)

2. When you exhale, open your hands as if to say, "It's out of my hands. This is going to be interesting because *my* ego is clearly not in control of this situation." (*Note:* practice this with your children, your parents, your boss, or your employees.)

3. Give yourself time to hold your breath and exhale at least three times. With each exhalation, let go of more tension and focus your attention on choosing to face the task before you as a fact of life, rather than cursing it or making it a problem. (*Note:* practice this when you're procrastinating on a project that some part of you doesn't want to do; remember, the self operates from *choice*—not "have to" or "want to.")

4. Consider feeling grateful for this challenge that takes you beyond your ego's perspective and puts you in touch with resources and support you didn't know you had. (*Note:* practice gratitude when paying the bills, facing a writing block, or wash-

ing the dishes; especially, be grateful for how your larger mind and self can calmly and creatively work with all aspects of life—even those aspects that you initially resist.)

In addition to the focused breath exercise, the following tips will also help you achieve optimal performance:

- Focus on just doing the job, not on judging your worth.
- Focus on what the task requires, not on trying to avoid criticism.
- Focus on human excellence, not on perfection.
- Focus on doing what you can do now, not on what another person does or what you think you should be able to do if the circumstances were ideal.
- Focus on difficult events and people as facts that you can coexist with, not as problems, obstacles, or enemies that you need to avoid, remove, or fight.
- Focus on *how* to clean up the spilled milk, not on *why* you spilled the milk.

9

Connection Replaces Lonely Struggle

Self in the Role of Coach

I have come to understand the extraordinary importance of leading an integrated life . . . of allowing myself to first notice, then to blend, all aspects of who I am—positive and . . . negative—into a grander Whole.

> —Neale Walsch, foreword to *The Dark Side of the Light Chasers* by Debbie Ford

CONNECTION, THE FIFTH QUALITY of your Strongest Self, activates the role of coach that empowers you to integrate all parts of yourself into an effective team. The quality of connection blends all parts into a grander whole so that no part of you is left stuck in the past, struggling alone. And you, as the self, are not alone either. In each of the roles of the self, you are empowered to connect to and support every part of yourself through your access to your subconscious mind, the integrated hemispheres of your brain, and your body's intuitive wisdom for survival. No part of you is ever alone, not even the self, nor should any single part of you—cognitive, emotional, or physical—ever take on the struggle of trying to manage your life alone.

It's worth summarizing the major premise of *Awaken Your Strongest Self*: The underlying cause of most of our problems is placing our identity in small, separate parts of ourselves and then allowing those parts to take charge of our lives. When we fail to put our Strongest Self and new brain in charge, our perspective is clouded by the dependency of childhood, the search for unconditional love, past failures and traumas, and overreliance on outdated, lower brain methods of coping.

The Magic of Connection

Allowing the separated parts to run your life would be like having the players of a sports team manage themselves without a coach. Regardless of the athletes' natural talents and their achievements in high school or college, they can't make it in the big leagues without a coach who can train them to think and play as members of a team.

That's what U.S. hockey coach Herb Brooks did in 1980 when his collection of American college kids forged themselves into a cooperative team and beat the Russian professionals who had won four straight Olympic gold medals. Against the odds that predicted certain defeat for the United States, a group of amateurs came together to form the winning (*Do You Believe in Miracles?*) team. In similar fashion the 2004 NBA championship was won by the underdog Detroit Pistons, a team with no superstars but with exceptional teamwork. The Pistons won their first title in fourteen years, defeating the favored Los Angeles Lakers by uniting all players into a cooperative team that avoided the distractions caused by conflicts among individual egos.

From the role, perspective, and voice of the coach, you can provide a strategic plan and vision that unites all players around a common purpose and finally puts you in charge of your own inner team. The separate egos—especially the "you have to" voice of the six-year-old and the "I don't want to" voice of the two-year-old—are no longer running your team. The executive organizing functions of your new brain are awake and asserting a vision to which all psychological, emotional, and physical parts of you can contribute.

The guidance you provide from the coach's perspective and wisdom wins you the loyalty and cooperation of the entire inner team. As you assume the role of coach, you may want to thank all the parts that have been trying to manage your life from their limited perspective. You may even want to apologize for not showing up earlier to relieve them of the unfair burden of taking charge of your life. You'll find it helpful to look inward and say to the overburdened, struggling parts of you, "I've finally shown up as the adult coach in my life. You no longer have to struggle alone. You can stop trying so hard to fix or change the past and your parents. You don't have to perform perfectly in order to be accepted. I'm on your side, regardless of success or failure. I will never abandon you. Regardless of your difficulties and flaws, I accept and love you completely."

In your notebook, you can add your own phrases of dialogue with the parts of you that have faithfully tried to protect you and cope with the early challenges in your life.

Letting Go of Lonely Struggle

Our Western culture and Puritan legacy teaches us that we must conquer nature in order to use our talents and attain our goals. It also tells us to try hard, struggle alone, and become rugged individualists. Many other cultures, however, seek to work in harmony with nature and in connection with the family and the community.

Those of us raised in a motorboat culture expect our technology, engines, and gasoline to bring us to our desired destination on time, in a straight line across the lake or sea. Acting as if we're separate from nature, we fail to learn how to harness the power of the tides and winds, and therefore, we perpetuate our dependence on external solutions such as mechanical devices and gasoline. Those raised in a sailboat society must learn how to work with nature by studying the wind, tides, and navigation by the stars. To reach their destination they must sail at an angle, tacking slightly away from their ultimate goal. Rather than demanding that they reach their goal directly, they enjoy the journey and their connection with the laws of nature.

Your life's journey will become considerably easier and more joyful when you stop struggling against life as if you're *apart from* it and start living as if you're *a part of* it and connected to it. While effort is required to produce advances in society and in your personal growth, struggle and striving are symptoms of the ego working alone, against nature—the laws of nature inside your own body and mind and in the larger universe.

Whenever I or my brother or sister would struggle to turn a faucet, bolt, or valve, my father would caution, "If you have to try hard to turn it, you're turning it in the wrong direction. It's supposed to be easy." When I was a child I didn't fully appreciate the wisdom of my father's words, but as I grew older I took them to heart. I've turned my father's practical philosophy into the following overarching principle in my own life: *Maximize the ease and joy of life. There's plenty of effort and work to go around; you don't need to add to it. If you're trying too hard, you're turning against life, going in the wrong direction.*

From the role and perspective of your Strongest Self, you can catch and connect with those parts of you that hold on to the illusion of separateness that keeps them trapped in a lonely struggle against life.

Moving from Struggle to Connection

To strengthen your physical memory of how to move from lonely struggle to connection, let's repeat some exercises. In the exercises that follow, notice what it feels like to work from a separated, struggling part of yourself. Notice the tension caused by trying harder and harder to do it all alone. Notice how quickly the burden is eased and the task made simple once you reconnect with your larger self and a deeper wisdom and support that goes beyond the understanding of your conscious mind or ego.

• Hold a briefcase or book at arm's length and notice how quickly your arm, acting on its own, separated from the rest of your body, tires of this struggle. Now bring your elbow to your hip—close to the area below the navel that the martial artists call *chi* or *ki* (as in Tai *Chi* Chuan or Ai*ki*do)—and notice how much easier it is to perform this task when your arm and every part of you is connected to your center.

• Try to open a heavy door with your arm fully extended from your body. Notice how hard your arm has to work when isolated from the rest of you. Then connect your elbow to your hip, grasp the doorknob, bend your knees slightly, connect your feet to the floor, and open the door by turning your body and hips. Notice how much easier and more gracefully you can open the door when all parts of you are connected and working together.

• Sit in a straight-back chair and imagine that your head and shoulders represent your ego identity separated from the rest of your body. Try to stand using only your head and shoulders to pull yourself up toward your goal of standing. It's almost impossible when your head is disconnected from the rest of your body, legs, and feet and the support of the floor. But notice how many times a day you attempt to lurch up and out of a chair at the risk of straining your lower back. (*Note:* do not attempt this exercise if you have problems with your knees.)

• Now imagine that your head—serving as a symbol for the ego—works with the support of your body and larger self. Your goal is still to move *up*, but this time you start by placing your attention on your feet and pressing them into the floor. Once you're connected to the floor through your feet, roll your head and shoulders *down* and forward, as if falling over your knees. Keep your head still and let your feet and legs support its weight while your spinal column uncoils—stacking one vertebra on top of another—until you're easily and safely out of the chair and standing up.

It may seem counterintuitive, but—as in many areas of life—in order to reach your objective, you must start by going in the opposite direction, away from your ultimate goal (the way a sailboat must tack on an angle to its destination). Instead of your head (or ego) acting alone and disconnected from the support of your body, connect it to your spine, your feet, and the floor, which represent the larger self and the support of nature and the earth.

Craig: Shifting Out of Struggle

As early as grammar school, Craig wanted to be perfect in order to avoid feeling shamed by his parents if he made a mistake or received any grade other than an A. Craig worked longer and harder on his homework assignments than anyone else in his class but, because of his anxiety, found it almost impossible to complete or hand in his work.

When his teachers sent reports home that said, "Craig is intelligent but lacks the motivation to complete his assignments," his parents were furious. They had to work hard to provide their son with the education and precious opportunities they never had. Their anger only added to Craig's perfectionism and confounded it with guilt, resentment, and a deeper sense of shame and worthlessness.

In spite of suffering from depression and self-doubt, Craig managed to get through high school with Bs and into a good college based on his ability to perform on standardized exams. In college Craig should have shown his true potential. But in fact, he was no longer the smartest kid in class and performed at the average level because of his worsening problem with completing his assignments. As his classes became more challenging, Craig found it nearly impossible to find the time necessary to keep up his standard of perfection that was supposed to make him invulnerable to criticism. His old ways of coping were grossly inadequate for coping with the pressures of advanced college courses. Craig had reached his limits and felt stuck in a self-defeating cycle. While therapy and medication helped somewhat, nothing seemed to help Craig break free of his old patterns. When he felt sick and tired of being out of control, he decided to call me for coaching.

At the start of our phone sessions, Craig was naturally skeptical that the Awaken Your Strongest Self program would work for him when nothing else had. But once he learned that he could shift out of the perspective of his struggling, perfectionist ego and connect to the deeper resources of his larger self, he became interested and hopeful that positive change was possible. After a few months of using the program, he sent me the following e-mail:

> Before our coaching sessions, I didn't realize that I was stuck in conflicting feelings of obligation to my parents and an uncontrollable need to be perfect. But the first few exercises helped me discover that there is an adult "I" that can choose what to do, regardless of the other voices and regardless of what others think. It was like being struck by lightning. Instead of feeling hesitant about what I'm going to do, I began to feel that I am strong enough to face the risks of handing in less-than-perfect work.
>
> I now clearly see and hear the younger parts of me and know that their voices come from a very lonely and isolated place in my childhood. For the first time in my life, I understand how my old solution of trying to be perfect was making things worse for so many years. Now I feel that I'm in charge of caring for myself, "accepting myself as perfectly human," and leading myself toward the completion of my goals. Now I have tools and resources—something I can work with and something that will work for me. It's great to know that I have alternative perspectives from which to view what's happening in my life that help me remain even-keeled.

> *You were right: it's more important for me to start and complete something that's imperfect than to hold on to a perfect fantasy that can never be completed.*

How the Voice of the Self Takes on the Role of Coach

Effective coaches observe their players to determine what they're doing that works and which habits and beliefs are keeping them from reaching their potential as individuals and team members. (Some of our high school and college coaches seem to believe in the ineffective coaching method of criticism and yelling. To refresh your memory on the steps involved in shifting to the voice of your Strongest Self, see Chapter 4.)

Keep in mind the "yes" template: "Yes . . . yes, of course . . . yes . . . and now I'm choosing what to do." That is, give at least three validations of your ego's emotions, fears, or beliefs before saying "and now" to make a bridge out of the past into the present. In stating "I will choose," the self is taking responsibility for its decisions and for the consequences of its actions.

Note that you are *not* asking the ego to give itself positive affirmations in order to feel strong enough to manage your life alone. You don't want your ego to struggle alone from its limited perspective, attempting to be in charge of your life. The voice of the self and the roles of the self initiate a shift to a stronger and more compassionate identity that unites all parts into a team effort.

In my seminars on stress and time management, I say to my audience, "How do you lead a horse out of a burning barn? The horse has a deep, instinctual fear of fire honed over millions of years. No amount of beating or pulling will make that horse walk through fire. You must turn the horse away from the fire, speak softly, pat the animal gently, cover its eyes, and then it will trust your leadership and follow you through the fire."

Whether you're talking to a horse—or to parts of you that have been struggling alone—you can speak in the voice of the effective trainer or coach and say the following:

- *Yes*, you believe you must struggle alone to survive and achieve. *Yes, of course* you don't trust that there's anyone else to help or support you. *Yes*, you have plenty of reasons to defend yourself and to fear enemies, problems, and hurts. *Yes*, you've been hurt by loss, criticism, and attacks.
- *And now I'm here*; you're not alone. Come here to connect with a deeper wisdom, safety, and peace. I will never abandon you. You'll always have a home here. I'm strong enough to be with your feelings. Regardless of what happens, I won't make you feel bad.
- *I'm choosing* what to do. I know better than any friend, lover, or therapist what you've been through. Even though you're worried, insecure, and imperfect, I accept and love you completely.

By learning to shift to the five major roles of your Strongest Self—protector, negotiator, leader, teacher, and coach—you've been shifting your sense of self toward a more expansive and stronger identity. In completing this four-step process, you might come to the same insights as if you had invested years in therapy or meditation: "I'm more than my thoughts, emotions, and impulses. I now know there's a calm, wise part of me that observes my emotions and my initial reactions and can choose to act in accord with my higher values and objectives. I'm no longer controlled by my obsolete reactions, fears, and the conditioned responses of my lower brains."

Ruth: Discovering a Self That Will Fight for Your Life

As a child Ruth was abused physically, psychologically, and sexually. She spent much of her life from the ages of twelve to thirty in despair, self-hatred, and drug abuse. By age forty, after undergoing years of therapy and recovery groups, Ruth came to my office to stop smoking and to end an abusive relationship.

Ruth's strong commitment to using this program to reclaim her life enabled her, in less than one year, to break her addiction to tobacco and to begin her first healthy relationship. To celebrate, Ruth planned a vacation in Hawaii—her first vacation in four years. In the midst of what most people consider paradise, she saw in greater contrast the pain of her past, became severely depressed, and was contemplating suicide.

While walking along an isolated beach, Ruth noticed that a man was following her. Despite her deep despair she felt an energizing anger welling up inside her. When the man approached and attempted to grab her, Ruth turned, kicked and punched him, and sent him away running. In an instant Ruth's deep feelings of depression and hopelessness had vanished. When she described to me her incredibly rapid shift in mood, she said, "I was about to throw my life away. But a strong part of me woke up and was ready to fight for my life. Discovering that I have this part of me saved my vacation—and maybe my life! Regardless of how depressed I feel in the future, I will always know that a split second away I have a central core of strength in me that will fight for my life."

Ruth is no longer stuck in the depression that a part of her felt—for some very legitimate reasons—about her past. She now knows that she is more than her past and her feelings of shame and despair. She keeps handy the miracle of shifting out of a deep despair to discover that she has a strong self that accepts her completely and will fight to protect her unique version of life—with all of its scars, joys, and challenges.

At times we all need to know that we have access to the expanded identity of a larger self that will fight for our life, regardless of the fears, self-doubts, or despair of our lesser parts. It's by learning to call upon this same self, every day—through ordinary disappointments, minor losses, and frustrations—that we ensure that we can access our larger, wiser, Strongest Self when confronting serious challenges or emergencies.

Exercise: Freeing Yourself from Bad Habits and Negative Thoughts

To break negative habits and detach from negative thoughts, you can keep handy—literally, at your fingertips—the commitment of yourself in the role of coach to protect your body and life. At least five times a day, take one minute to do the following exercise, adapted from Drs. Herbert and David Spiegel's book *Trance and Treatment*.

Use three-part breathing in three breaths:

1. Inhale and, while keeping your chin level, roll your eyes upward as far as you can, with your eyelids opened or closed.
2. Hold your breath while continuing to look up.
3. Exhale slowly and completely, letting your eyes roll forward and down as you concentrate on the feeling of floating down into the chair and into the floor.

You may notice a profound relaxation flowing down your body as you let your eyes relax and float down and as you look inward to make a commitment to your body and your life. In three breaths, each in three parts, say one of the following statements to yourself:

- **First breath.** "This is my life and my body—working for me like a faithful servant twenty-four hours a day, every day." (You can lift your thumb to indicate this first statement.)
- **Second breath.** "Certain habits, beliefs, substances, and relationships are toxic to my body and the full experience of my life and its potential." (You can bring your first finger and thumb together to indicate the joining of your first and second statements.)
- **Third breath.** "I am committed to protecting my life and my body from all toxic habits, beliefs, substances, and relationships in

order to experience my full vitality and potential." (Join your middle finger to your thumb and first finger and press them together to signal a firm commitment.)

Then as you exhale, release the pressure of your thumb and fingers and softly open your eyes.

Whenever you say these statements, or press your thumb and first and second fingers together, you are reasserting your role as a strong, protective self that is committed to protecting your life and your body. You can name specific habits (such as smoking or overeating) and toxic substances (such as tobacco and fattening foods). A client who has used this exercise wrote, "I found the pressing together of my fingers is quite effective in helping me feel support and strength. It's amazing how powerful such seemingly simple actions can be."

Exercise for Chapter 9: Centering Within Your Larger Self

Physical activities such as sports, dance, and the martial arts can serve as physical metaphors for learning how to make psychological and behavioral changes in other arenas in your life. They give you an opportunity to observe—in relatively safe settings—how the focus of your attention, your beliefs, and your emotional states can affect your enjoyment of an activity and the achievement of your goals.

Commitments to walk, hike, swim, or do aerobics, for example, can show you that even when one part of you wants to quit, your larger, integrated self has much more endurance than your ego can imagine.

A nonaggressive martial art such as Aikido or Tai Chi will provide immediate physical feedback to tell you when you have allowed outside pressures to throw your attention—and thus your body—off balance. To recover balance you need to know when your mind is distracted by fear, is struggling to achieve a goal, or is just not paying attention to the present. A daily practice will strengthen your access to your larger self and provide directions to lead you back home after one of your negative coping patterns has led you astray.

In the following exercise—adapted from Wendy Palmer's book *The Practice of Freedom*—you and a partner stand opposite each other. As Morihei Ueshiba, founder of this martial art, has said, "The secret of Aikido is to harmonize ourselves with the movement of the universe and bring ourselves into accord with the universe itself. He who has gained the secret of Aikido has the universe in himself and can say, 'I am the universe.'"

1. Center yourself—feet apart, left foot forward with knee slightly bent, right foot back with knee straight—and then have your partner extend his or her right arm and push on your left shoulder.

2. Notice your reaction to pressure. This is your initial, or default, defensive reaction. Do you instantly push back as if your partner were a problem, an enemy, or an obstacle? Do you collapse under pressure? Without judgment, just make note of your body's automatic response patterns. Also notice the thoughts and images that occupy your mind.

3. Shift your attention from the pressure on your shoulder (a metaphor for stress or a problem) to your hips, where you can connect with the support of your legs, your feet, and the floor. Note that you are shifting from the default reactions of your body and mind to a larger sense of self that is connected to deeper support from within your body and from the earth.

4. Your partner's job is to keep pressure on you and then to quickly release the pressure. If your attention is truly centered on connecting to your inner strength and mission, rather than on fighting the supposed problem or enemy, you'll remain balanced. If your attention is on opposing the supposed problem or enemy, you'll fall forward when the pressure is released. Remember, your mission and your inner resources should be more interesting than the other person or your initial reactions.

5. Repeatedly recenter, deeper into yourself and the support behind you and below you, as your partner adds more pressure and then releases. Notice how placing attention on your hips, your legs, and the support of the earth shifts you from fighting against the pressure to connecting with the larger strength within you and the deeper support all around you.

When you center within your Strongest Self, you can deal with more pressure more easily. When you are in harmony with the universe, there are no problems, only facts. Some facts require you to connect to, and become, a stronger, larger fact.

Awaken the Leader in You to Achieve Your Goals

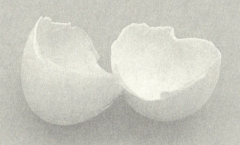

10

Self-Efficacy and the Stages of Change

The Key to Realizing Your Dreams

The capacity to exercise control over one's own functioning and the events that affect one's life is the essence of humanness.
—Albert Bandura, *Self-Efficacy: The Exercise of Control*

WHEN YOU TAKE CHARGE of the direction of your life and make things happen, you're using your brain's higher functions of planning and self-regulation to turn your dreams into reality. When you intend to complete a task and then actually complete it, you're exercising the self-leadership skills that bring you what researchers call self-efficacy.

You feel confident and capable and achieve a sense of satisfaction and high self-esteem.

To manage your life effectively you need the cooperation and contribution of all parts of yourself to create the grander whole of who you truly are. Imagine that your various, often conflicting, inner voices are members of a committee with your Strongest Self as the chairperson who facilitates the inner discussion. When you call a "committee meeting," in which all parts are heard, you eliminate self-sabotage, resistance, and worry while maximizing your chances of achieving your goals and attaining inner peace. Playing the role of an orchestra conductor or a committee chairperson will enable you to integrate all parts of your personality into a harmonious team, thus avoiding overidentification with any single part of you. In an integrated team approach to taking charge of your life, it's your Strongest Self that takes full responsibility for the final decisions, especially when something unexpected or painful occurs.

Resistance and self-sabotage are minimized because the participation and commitment of every member of the committee is called for before you take action. With a shared vision, the cooperation of every team member is more likely. When the self takes responsibility for the risks involved in any decision, the lesser parts can relax their fears and their tendency to be overly worried about mistakes that could cause the loss of approval from authority figures. They've performed their duties of alerting you to survival concerns; you've heard them, reassured them of internal safety, and made executive decisions about what to do.

How I Went from Inner Conflict to Inner Peace

Before I was diagnosed with terminal cancer at the age of thirty-two, I thought my feelings, behaviors, and patterns were unchangeable parts of who I was. For example, I was self-righteous about my smoking, my tendency to work without stopping, my impatience, and my aggressive driving. When my fiancée would ask me to change these habits, I would become defensive and argue that she was asking me to change who I was as a person. After my cancer diagnosis I began to see that my reactions, thoughts, and habits had to change if I was to have the best possible chance of living to see thirty-four. My new attitude and habits would have to be strong enough to survive a journey that included surgery, innumerable medical tests, eighteen months of chemotherapy, and possibly radiation.

With a 10 percent chance to live one year, the odds were clearly against me. I was determined not to waste what might be the last year of my life in fear, passively following doctor's orders or making myself feel bad. I was waking up to a protective role toward my life and my body. Empowered by my protective role, I fired the first surgeon and agreed to work with another, who performed exploratory surgery, which confirmed that I did have metastasized cancer. I had resisted what I thought would be unnecessary surgery for more than two weeks and was strangely relieved to discover that it was necessary. I had not made a mistake by submitting to my doctor's pressure to have surgery.

I was relieved because I escaped the fury of some part of me that would make me feel miserable if I had made a mistake. I was shocked to discover that I was afraid of incurring my own wrath for not being perfect! (I named this part of me the dictator.) This is step 1 of the Awaken Your Strongest Self program. I had identified a part of me that I would need to integrate into my larger self if I was going to maintain some remnant of inner peace during the months of chemotherapy that lay before me. Newly awakened to playing a leadership role in my life, I found my sense of mission and values to have become clearer. If I was going to maximize my chances of survival, every part of me needed to be aligned with that mission and those values. Every part of me—even the dictator—needed to contribute to my values of inner peace, minimal stress, and acting from choice rather than the inner conflict of "you have to" versus "I don't want to." I would not let the dictator voice make any part of me feel bad or cause stress by making threats.

Uniting All Parts into a Grander Whole

Following surgery to remove the cancerous tumor, I found a doctor who agreed with me that chemotherapy—instead of more surgery—made sense in my case. He told me that for nine months I would take a weekly dose of a very strong chemotherapy cocktail, followed by a year of monthly doses to ensure that they had completely eradicated this very virulent cancer from my body.

It was this longer fight that taught me the most about the qualities necessary for uniting all parts of myself around my objectives and values. With chemotherapy taking a large toll on my energy, I had to choose what to get upset about and what to let go if I expected to continue working, tolerate the full treatment, and have energy for evenings with friends or to write about my cancer experience. This journey was too big for me to take alone. I needed to connect with a larger sense of self within me—something larger than my ego and intellect that could unite the wisdom of my mind, body, and intuition. I needed the help of friends and professionals to deal with the setbacks, upsets, and discouragement.

After the first nine months, the schedule of chemotherapy treatments changed from weekly to monthly, and only then could I experience their real effects on my body. After each chemotherapy treatment, I felt as if I had the flu or pneumonia for two weeks. Then my energy would return so that I could even jog a few miles, before having another treatment and starting the cycle of weakness and fatigue all over again. I rode this emotional and physical roller coaster for nine more months before asking my doctor, "What if I stop now?" He answered that I should continue chemotherapy for at least six to nine more months. But because I had lived for eighteen months beyond the diagnosis, the odds had reversed, and there was now a 90 percent chance that I was cured.

Acknowledging the "What If" Voice

That evening I sat in my living room with a pen and a pad of paper and convened a committee meeting of all my inner voices. I closed my eyes, turned my head down as if looking inward, and told every part of me that I was about to end chemotherapy unless the doctor could convince me to continue. I considered what I had asked my body to go through for eighteen months, and I considered the risks of stopping chemotherapy against the recommendation of my doctor.

I realized that I could not stop treatment just because some part of me didn't want the pain and disruption chemotherapy caused me. I knew that I couldn't continue just because some part of me was afraid of making a mistake by not following orders. Regardless of which direction I chose, I knew every part of me would have to be committed to the mission.

On my pad I wrote down what came to me about every possible worry, risk, benefit, and criticism I would face if my decision to stop chemotherapy proved to be a mistake to my family, my doctor, and me. I imagined each scenario and acknowledged each what if, including "What if the cancer comes back?" Most frequently I responded with, "Yes, that would be awful. Yes, that would really hurt. Yes, I'd probably cry and be upset. . . . And I won't let it last for long. I'm taking full responsibility for this decision. I can live with the consequences."

During that committee meeting I realized that the dictator part of me that had revealed itself at the time of my surgery a year and a half earlier had truly been integrated into my larger self. Now there was barely any fear of making a mistake. There was no doubt that I—acting as my Strongest Self—was in charge and could minimize the self-criticism if the cancer came back or if I had the thought that I'd made a mistake. The dictator was gone or had been transformed into a helpful member of my team. And *I* certainly was transformed over those eighteen months of chemotherapy. That night, seated in the chairperson's role for more than an hour, I reached a new level of integration. It was both calming and empowering to feel that I had a complete team behind my decision to stop chemotherapy.

At my next meeting with the doctor, he tested my resolve, saying, "I'm responsible for your life. You don't need to make these kinds of decisions." Two years earlier I would have prayed for someone or something outside of me to take responsibility for my life, but now I was speaking up for the committee of selves. I was in a leadership role and empowered to tell the doctor with conviction, "I will consider your advice, Doctor, but only *I* can be responsible for my life. After all, I'm the one who will live or die with the consequences of these decisions."

I ended chemotherapy that day and lived to write about it in *The Road Back to Health: Coping with the Emotional Aspects of Cancer*. This was not a cavalier decision. I had already had surgery and had withstood nine months of weekly chemotherapeutic agents and another nine months of monthly treatments. Chemotherapy saved my life. But it was time to give my body a chance on its own. My committee and I could live with that decision.

Conducting a "Committee Meeting" to Resolve Conflict

Holding a "committee meeting" with the various parts of yourself can resolve inner conflict, indecisiveness, and worry in just a few minutes. What makes these meetings more powerful and effective than your usual inner dialogue is that you—as the self in the role of the chairperson—state your vision and objectives and then invite all other parts to state their concerns. Instead of arguing with the worrying and fearful parts of you, you listen, take their concerns under advisement, and let them tell you what they need in order to fully cooperate and contribute.

One of my clients thinks of the committee meeting as a potluck in which every part brings its specialty, along with its unique perspective and concerns. She especially wants to hear from the "what if" and the "yes, but what if we fail?" voices. She also encourages all parts of herself to bring their enthusiasm, energy, and deep longing to be part of a larger sense of purpose.

Once objections and concerns about past failures have been addressed, support for the self's leadership vision is garnered. In order to create an integrated team effort, cooperation must replace inner conflict, and active commitment must replace passive compliance. The following steps will help you conduct your own committee meeting:

1. Sit comfortably with your eyes closed and look inward. Visualize a meeting in which you are in the chairperson's seat and role. Take at least three breaths to float down into the support of the chair and to let go of muscle tension.

2. State your goals, vision, and mission to all those assembled, and invite their cooperation and contribution. For example, say, "I want to lose twenty pounds. I'm committed to making exercise a regular part of my week. I'm committed to protecting my body from its addictive habits. I'm no longer using food as a drug or a solution to all problems. Food and eating will no longer occupy my mind as if they're the answer to everything. I want your cooperation in achieving these goals."

3. Invite all parts to express their cooperation, resistance, or concerns. As with any meeting, you can expect some members to say, "We tried that and it didn't work. What if it backfires like last time and you gain weight, get depressed, and hate yourself?"

4. Answer all what ifs with the "yes" template (see Chapter 4). For example, *Yes*, it would be very upsetting if that happened. *Yes, of course* it would hurt. *Yes*, that would be awful. *And I would choose* to accept and forgive myself, get help, and start again. If that happens I will not let it ruin our weekend. I have a plan for bouncing back. And my overall plan is, regardless of what happens, I will not make you feel bad.

5. Ask, "What do you need to hear from me in order to fully cooperate and participate in achieving this goal?" (The usual

responses require you to act as a leader who provides safety, acts from choice, protects every part from criticism, and has a plan to recover from disappointment and setbacks.)

Once the larger self acting in the role of chairperson provides the five qualities—safety, choice, presence, focus, and connection—that replace the five major problems, all parts will generally cooperate and follow your lead. It's not unusual, however, to need a few more committee meetings or brief daily discussions to keep the team focused on your mission and to maintain the total cooperation of every part.

With persistent problems, such as procrastination or difficult and worrisome challenges, gather together all the usual suspects—the rebel voice, the dictator, the worrier, the people pleaser, and all fearful parts—every day for a brief committee meeting of five to ten minutes to reconsider your issues and goals. You'll learn that spending a few minutes integrating all parts of yourself makes it possible to eliminate ambivalence, procrastination, and self-sabotage, thereby allowing you to make considerable progress in achieving your goals. The increase in your energy and motivation gained from a cooperative effort can be remarkable. Seemingly immovable blocks can disappear when all parts of you are pulling together in a team effort.

Effective Goal Setting

During a series of presentations I was giving at Rancho La Puerta in Mexico, I joined a family for dinner on the night I was to speak about effective goal setting. Their four-year-old daughter, Stacy, asked me what I was going to talk about. I told her my speech was about how to make wishes come true. Stacy brightened and said, "Oh, I know how to do that. You find the first star that comes out, you make your wish upon it, and then you go to sleep. When you wake up, it comes true."

That night Stacy made the first of what I'm sure has become many presentations before an audience. When I asked her if she wanted to tell her wishing upon a star method to my audience, she jumped at the chance and told the audience how to make effective wishes. But she had added an additional element to effective goal setting that I would've left out—you must go to sleep. That is, your conscious mind must let go of the goal so your subconscious can work on it in your night- and daydreams.

Your conscious mind and ego must stop trying so hard and learn to go from worry to wonder in order to access the genius of the subconscious, dreaming mind. The ego needs to learn that it must be a team player if it's to contribute to the mission of working more easily, more creatively, and with greater joy. You must guide your ego toward connection with the rest of the team, which includes the genius of the subconscious mind and the wisdom of the body, as well as the leadership vision of your Strongest Self.

Typical goal setting is nothing more than your ego's wish list of wants and New Year's resolutions. It's a one-step process that sets the ultimate goal or wished-for objective and then stops there. Without the self's *choice* and *commitment*, such wants will most likely result in procrastination, failure, self-criticism, and decreased motivation.

The Rules of Behavior Change

An essential tool that contributes to your enhanced ability to achieve your goals and maintain healthy habits is an understanding of the mechanisms and probabilities of behavior change. To make this program something more than a gamble with your hopes, energy, and dreams, you need to know the rules of the game. In the game of habit change, an immediate reward always wins over a distant and indefinite reward, unless you have a leadership vision, a strong commitment, and a strategy for improving the odds for long-term habit change. In other words, without the leadership of your higher brain and your Strongest Self, the odds are against changing a habit or a conditioned reaction.

If you hope to be in charge of your habits, it's essential to understand that your lower brains' survival programs and habitual behaviors are controlled by immediate and definite consequences (rewards or punishments). Without guidance and regulation from your awakened higher brain, you're less likely to achieve goals that have distant and indefinite rewards. The odds are in favor of today's countless sources of more immediate gratification that will consume your attention, time, and resources. See the following chart for a diagram of those tasks, goals, and habits that have a low or high chance of occurring because of the proximity and certainty of their rewards and punishments.

What Are the Consequences of Your Behavior?

Task, Goal, or Habit	Immediate and Definite Consequences	Distant and Indefinite Possible Consequences	Chance of Occurrence
changing diet or increasing amount of exercise	discomfort, self-criticism, fear	weight loss? fitness? high self-esteem?	low
working hard or studying hard	loneliness, self-criticism, frustration	pay raise? grade of A? high self-esteem?	low
goofing off at work or in school	fun, reduction of tension and fear	get fired? grade of F? low self-esteem?	high
watching TV or surfing Internet	fun, reduction of tension and fear	weight gain? illness? low self-esteem?	high

Can you predict what you will do in the next twenty-four hours? Are you willing to bet a hundred dollars that you will run five miles, stop eating by 8 P.M., empty out the garage or spare room, clean the house, paint the living room, or learn the tax codes? Or are you more likely to bet that you'll watch TV, eat dessert, check e-mail, talk on the phone, take a nap, or read a magazine? The odds are clearly in favor of accomplishing the simple and immediately pleasurable tasks against starting the more complex tasks whose rewards are in the distant future.

Because the negative consequences of goofing off and overeating are in the distant future and uncertain—you *may* get fired from your job or earn a grade of F, and you *may* gain twenty pounds—they have little effect on your current decisions.

That's why it's important to learn how to "feel the pain of staying the same" when you want to eliminate a negative, problematic habit. When you want to achieve a positive goal, it's helpful to instill persistence over a long period of time by experiencing in the present some of the success of your future achievements while lessening the discomfort, loneliness, and self-criticism.

To increase your chances of achieving the goals that make a real, long-term difference in your life and provide the greatest rewards and levels of satisfaction, you need a plan for how you'll deal with the challenges you'll encounter along the path to your goal. Without engaging these higher brain functions, the odds are that you will only do those things—such as snacking, chatting on the phone, or surfing the Web—that give you immediate pleasure or allow you to temporarily escape the self-doubt, loneliness, and anxiety that often accompany larger tasks whose rewards are in the distant future.

To achieve a long-term goal—one that requires you to face your fears and start working now—you must lessen the immediate discomfort caused by self-criticism, self-threats, and pressure and bring the future rewards into your current imagery and experience. Breaking a large project into small, success-assured steps also helps lower discomfort, builds confidence, and gives you more immediate satisfaction. To continue to pursue a goal over many months or years, you'll need to be able to taste, see, and grasp some part of the distant reward. As I write in *The Now Habit: Overcoming Procrastination While Enjoying Guilt-Free Play*, you need to reward yourself for all the small steps along the path to your long-term goals. You can put guilt-free playtime into your schedule—thereby making it legitimate—and use it as an immediate reward for brief, focused periods of work.

Making Your Dreams Come True—in Stages

By using the committee meeting approach to respond to the self-doubts and fears of all your respective parts, and by gaining their cooperation, you avoid the inner conflict and ambivalence that leads to only halfhearted attempts at goal achievement. The skills you've been gaining have equipped you with an enhanced ability to achieve your goals and change your habits from the perspective of your Strongest Self rather than from an overwhelmed, struggling ego. Learning to integrate all parts of you by conducting a committee meeting will help you complete the first of the four stages of effective change presented in the next four chapters. These research-based stages increase your chances of achieving your goals and maintaining healthy habits, such as more frequent exercise and proper diet.

If you've ever tried to lose weight, stop smoking, or made New Year's resolutions to exercise and live a more balanced life, you know how difficult—and, often, disheartening—it can be to repeatedly set goals and then fail at achieving them. Such failures often are followed by the unproductive tactic of self-criticism for being lazy, lacking motivation, or just being an awful person who has no willpower. While constructive criticism can be helpful, self-blame usually lowers motivation and interrupts your ability to learn from mistakes and take corrective action. In fact, your prior failures may be the result of simply skipping an essential stage in the process of successful change and goal achievement.

Don't despair. There's still hope even if your efforts at habit change have failed in the past. In the last twenty years the National Institutes of Health and the fields of behavioral medicine and health psychology have extensively researched what it takes to successfully achieve and maintain health goals and habits. Government and university researchers have shown that successful change takes place in four main stages. Skipping any one of these stages lowers the odds of successful, long-term improvement.

Their studies of the stages of change have made the process, if not easy, more predictable, understandable, and doable. In research with people from several countries, they've found that following the stages of change can help people improve diet, increase the frequency of exercise, and stop smoking. I've applied their models for effective change to a wide variety of client goals, such as losing weight, increasing productivity, overcoming procrastination, and enhancing skills in sports and musical performances.

Remember, you have an advantage over those who attempt to adapt new habits and eliminate destructive patterns using only a small, separate part of themselves. You've been discovering that your Strongest Self doesn't have to wait for the smaller parts of you to feel confident and motivated before you start the process of positive change and transformation. When you combine what you've been learning and practicing in the Awaken Your Strongest Self process with the stages of effective change, you'll find that your goal achievement program is under new management. Your Strongest Self—not your overwhelmed, fearful ego—will be integrating your conscious and subconscious resources to guide you inexorably toward a more joyful and fulfilling life in which you can turn your dreams into reality.

From the current research I've adapted four stages of change (see Figure 10.1 on the next page):

Stage I: Making Up Your Mind (the first, precommitment stage)
Stage II: Committing to Change
Stage III: Taking Action
Stage IV: Maintaining Long-Term Success

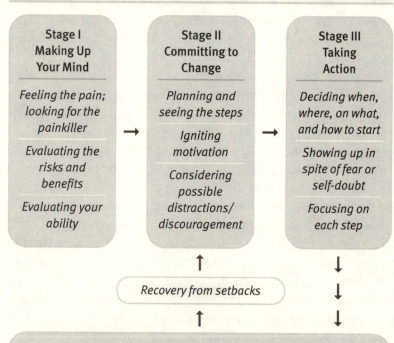

FIGURE 10.1 Stages of Effective Change

Stage I of the effective change process starts with you evaluating the pros and cons of change, reducing your self-doubts, and building confidence and motivation before you decide if and when you'll commit to changing your habits. Programs that fail to achieve long-term habit change usually skip Stage I, in which you build confidence in yourself and in the belief that there really is a solution that could work for you. Ineffective programs also tend to skip Stage IV, in which you prepare a plan for recovering from setbacks. Hundreds of research studies reveal that to be successful in changing your health habits, you need to take time to fully commit to the path to the goal (Stages I and II) and have a plan for dealing with challenges along the way before taking action (Stage III). These studies also reveal that to maintain healthy habits for the long term, you must prepare for setbacks and rehearse getting back on track (Stage IV). By following the four stages of change, not only are you more likely to achieve your goals for the long run, but you'll be better prepared to bounce back from normal setbacks.

Whether your dream is to complete years of training for your career, to stop smoking, to buy your first home, or to recover from a life-threatening illness or accident, it can be too much for you—or your ego or conscious mind—to confront these monumental challenges alone. To live optimally—and, at times, to just survive—you'll need to gain the cooperation of all parts of yourself in supporting and contributing to your vision. You'll need access to the creative resources of your integrated left- and right-brain hemispheres and your conscious and subconscious minds under the leadership of your Strongest Self. In these final chapters you'll put your leadership skills and roles to use to ensure that every part of you will want to be a part of, and contribute to, your vision.

11

Stage I

Making Up Your Mind

Nothing is so fatiguing as the eternal hanging on of an uncompleted task.

—William James

IT MAY SOUND SIMPLE, but in this first stage you can actually consider not changing. You don't have to change and you don't even have to believe that you are capable of overcoming long-standing destructive or outdated patterns. Your current situation may be comfortable, even satisfying. There may be no sense of urgency to make changes in your life at this time. If you're willing to live with the consequences, you don't have to meet the deadlines for your projects, get a root canal, stop smoking, fix the roof, or change your diet. It's your choice and your responsibility. And it is you—not the parts of you that are fearful and ambivalent— who will pay the price or reap the rewards.

In order to fully choose an overwhelming, costly, or lengthy project such as losing twenty pounds, writing a grant proposal, or stopping smoking, you must give yourself the option of not having to do it. Only then can you be sure that you're making a higher brain, higher self *choice* that's neither a have to nor simply a want to. Your ego doesn't have to want to do something that's difficult for your Strongest Self to *choose* to take the action necessary to preserve your health, keep your job, or avoid difficulties with the IRS. When we say, "I have no choice," we usually are indicating that we aren't willing to face the consequences of our choices or aren't willing to accept the alternatives that are available. We—or our inner critic and dictator—insist on having things our way or else, with the implied threat: "I will make myself miserable if I don't get what I want. I don't want to have to look for a new job or a new partner or give up my favorite foods and habits."

Our choices are not always easy or pleasant, but our Strongest Self can make those tough choices regardless of the doubts, resistance, and fears of some smaller part of us. We can choose surgery and chemotherapy to remove disease from our bodies, and we can learn to exercise in order to maintain health and prevent disease. Just as it's a characteristic of the human spirit to overcome its animal fear of fire, it's also an assertion of your humanness to face difficulty for a higher purpose rather than to simply seek short-term pleasure and avoid discomfort.

Warning: It's Dangerous to Remain Undecided!

When I was unhappy about my weight but not doing anything about it, I used to get into a cycle of criticizing myself, feeling more unhappy and helpless, and then eating more sweets and snacks in an attempt to eradicate these painful emotions. The more unhappy, lonely, discouraged, or bored I felt, the more I became self-critical and sought an immediate—though temporary—painkiller. The most available and quick painkillers usually involved unhealthy choices, such as drinking, smoking, and sitting in front of the computer or television for hours while consuming an extra thousand calories of snacks. At such times it never occurred to me to take a walk, go to the gym, eat an apple, or—heaven forbid!—deal with my emotions.

That was my primitive coping style before I awakened my Strongest Self and put it in a leadership role. Now I can see how not changing my pattern of consuming thousands of unneeded calories caused me to gain ten to fifteen pounds over five years. If I were to do nothing in the next five years to change this pattern, I'd gain another ten to twenty extra pounds and be five years older. And exercising would become increasingly more difficult and unappealing. I *wanted* to lose twenty pounds in one year—it was a *wish* and my annual New Year's resolution—but I wasn't fully *committed* to the process of change. I knew I wanted the goal but was not ready to commit to the long and perilous path leading to that goal. Because the negative consequences of my negative habits wouldn't be felt or seen for months or years, I could easily delude myself that my diet was fine and that I deserved a treat now and then. Of course, I'd completely forget about all the treats I had already given myself.

In order to commit to a long-term process of exercising and eating less sugar and carbohydrates, I needed to learn how to deal with uncomfortable feelings rather than trying to drug them away. I learned that my behavior is more strongly influenced by immediate consequences than by distant rewards (as you may recall from "The Rules of Behavior Change" in Chapter 10). To give healthy habits a fighting chance over destructive habits that bring immediate gratification, therefore, I needed to feel, more immediately, the pain that would result from continuing the same unhealthy patterns.

Exercise: Imagine Five Years Have Passed—Feel the Pain of Staying the Same

Consider the risks of staying the same for the next five years. Imagine that five years have passed and you're looking back on what's happened. Say to yourself, "Five years have passed. It's the year 20___ and I'm ___ years old. Very little has changed in my life during the last five years. I'm still working on the same goals, facing the same problems, living in the same place, working at the same job, and struggling with the same relationship issues." Now answer these questions:

1. How do you feel about your situation?

2. What absolutely must change in less than five years? Write down what must change and how soon (for example, in three months, six months, or one year).

3. Look back over the last five years to see if you're still dealing with the same problems and goals as you were then. If you haven't made changes in the last five years, consider the negative results of continuing this pattern for another five years. Will you gain another ten pounds, increase your risk of heart disease or cancer, or lose your ability to be active? Will you still be working at the same job on the same projects and feel frustrated and angry with yourself?

4. Identify what's keeping you from considering a plan to make changes in your life. Remember, you're not committing to change nor are you taking action. You're merely considering what you need to know and feel in order to state your intention to change. You're still at Stage I, making up your mind about the risks and benefits of change and wondering when you'll be ready for Stage II, committing to change.

Having a Clear Image of Future Pain

The anticipation of pain can motivate us to face present-day discomfort to avoid future unpleasantness. This simple but unpleasant fact was affirmed in experiments conducted by myself and my colleagues when we attempted to increase our own productivity in writing grants and proposals. Penalties such as payments of twenty dollars for failure to meet a deadline spurred some effort but were not powerful enough to consistently bring results. What worked was a contract to clean a friend's apartment for three to five hours on a Saturday if in thirty days we didn't complete some part of a major project (for example, writing a chapter of a paper, breaking off a dead-end relationship, or completing last year's income tax).

A clear image of future pain strengthens our determination to face our current fear and ambivalence. This technique has worked in every case for those who were willing to make the commitment in writing. Amazingly, each participant actually accomplished forty to sixty hours of high-quality work in one month rather than spend three hours cleaning someone else's home! When we thought about watching television instead of doing the work in front of us, the clear image of cleaning someone else's apartment on the weekend motivated us to choose to do some work instead of goofing off.

Both tasks may be unpleasant, but our mind compares the levels of discomfort, making the least unpleasant task seem more appealing. I call this strategy creative procrastination. If I've been procrastinating on my to-do list, I find another task that is bigger and more unpleasant and put it on top of the list. I then find myself procrastinating on it and completing the rest of my to-do list more quickly.

What if You Lack Motivation or Confidence?

Feeling ineffective and losing faith in your ability to achieve your goals can lead to frustration, procrastination, and low self-esteem. Lacking motivation and self-confidence is not a normal state for human beings. It's a sign that both your physical and psychological energies are depressed because of illness, repeated failures, social or environmental obstacles, or an ineffective plan for advancing toward your goals. Even if a part of you doesn't feel ready to make changes now, you probably feel—both consciously and subconsciously—some need to advance your life and make circumstances better for others. Despite our conditioning in the Puritan and Victorian beliefs that humans are lazy and we therefore must be threatened and coerced into getting motivated to improve our lives, there's a part of our human nature that is determined to learn more, achieve more, and reach higher levels of awareness and aliveness.

Goal setting, motivation, curiosity for new knowledge, and a desire for self-mastery are as natural in the human species as an infant's drive to leave behind the comfort of crawling for the risks and excitement of standing and walking on his or her own two feet. As Dr. Abraham Maslow, the founder of humanistic psychology, has said, "We have a higher nature which includes the need for meaningful work, for responsibility, for creativeness, for being fair and just, for doing what is worthwhile, and for preferring to do it well." In other words, we're naturally motivated to improve our mind, our health, and our home and community. When you seem to lack motivation, something's blocking this innate drive. As proposed here, a major block to transformative change is overidentifying with a smaller, more primitive part of yourself, thereby underestimating the resources you have as an integrated, Strongest Self.

Your brain is designed to be an effective dreamer and a creative problem solver. When you're effective in achieving your goals, you know your awakened Strongest Self is playing its proper leadership role and guiding you through numerous obstacles and self-doubts to the realization of your vision.

Angela: Lacking Confidence in Stage I

When twenty-nine-year-old Angela, a single administrative assistant, came to my office, she'd already spent a small fortune on three weight-control programs that failed to help her achieve her goals to stop binge eating, lose forty-five pounds, and reduce her risk of diabetes. These programs did not provide her with tools to cope effectively with the daily stress of her job, her demanding boss, and her wish to support her sick mother and younger siblings. Overeating and binging became her default methods for trying to comfort herself and lower her stress. Understandably, she wasn't confident that another program could help her succeed in changing her long-standing habits, but she was willing to give it one more try.

It became clear to me that before she even tried to achieve her goals, Angela would need to find healthy alternatives to stress, inner conflict, self-criticism, and feeling overwhelmed and disconnected from a larger support system. She needed to learn how to awaken her Strongest Self to experience the five qualities of safety, choice, presence, focus, and connection in her life. I told Angela that before we began any program of habit change, we would start with the Awaken Your Strongest Self program to ensure that she wasn't repeating the pattern of allowing some small part of her to cope alone with trying to achieve her goals.

On hearing this, Angela relaxed some of her fear that she was about to fail at yet another attempt to lose weight and to stop destructive ways of coping with overwhelming stress. Within five sessions Angela grasped the concept of awakening the compassionate voice of her Strongest Self and learned how to identify her habitual responses to stress, frustration, and loneliness. She then was ready to start a new, research-based four-stage program of change from a completely new perspective and with the cooperation of every part of herself. We used some questions to help her make up her mind about starting a new program. Later in this chapter and in the next few chapters, you'll find out how Angela used the four stages of change to implement her plans and achieve her goals.

Questions to Help You Build Confidence and Self-Esteem

Angela and I devised a few simple questions for her to ask herself to determine her level of confidence. After stating each question, she gave herself a few moments to notice the responses that came to her. You may want to do the same, changing the issue to fit your goals. Overeating and binging are used here as examples of difficult habits to change, because you can't completely stop eating the way you can completely stop smoking cigarettes. To eat just enough without overindulging or binging, you must be mindful of your emotional triggers and find ways of nurturing yourself with internal messages of acceptance rather than with dependence on external fixes.

To start her on the process of making up her mind about committing to another program of positive habit change, I instructed Angela to eat as she usually does without trying to change anything during this first stage. She was to just notice how she ate—like a person not obsessed with food or dieting—without the pressure to constantly watch what she was eating as if she were on a diet. She began by asking herself the following questions:

Question: Can I just notice, for two weeks, my thoughts about binging and my cravings for sweet and fattening food?

Answer: Yes, and I like that there's no pressure to make changes. I believe I can just notice.

Question: Can I pause and take one breath after I notice a thought or craving about binging?

Answer: Yes, I think I can do that.

Question: Can I just notice, during my one breath, the feelings associated with thoughts about eating and binging?

Answer: Yes. I want to learn how to do that.

For two weeks Angela noticed her thoughts about food and her impulses to binge, and she kept a journal of what was happening emotionally when they occurred. She noticed that her usual feelings—anxiety, stress, and loneliness—quickly led to thoughts about eating her favorite comfort foods and planning when to binge. She said, "I was amazed at how often I think about food. It's as if there's a giant neon sign flashing in my brain that says, 'Eat!' Watching those thoughts makes them seem like random noises that happen throughout the day. I think it will be easier to ignore most of those thoughts except when I'm upset about my family and when I feel lonely."

In answering these questions Angela was, in effect, asking the worrying, fearful part of her if these small steps could be taken without creating panic, fear of failure, or a feeling of being overwhelmed. She discovered that some part of her was able to say, "Yes, I can do this small step." If her answer were no to any of the questions, we'd ask questions that offered smaller steps. Keeping a journal made Angela aware of when her cravings and binging occurred. She said, "I tend to binge when I'm nervous, lonely, or stressed and I want someone or something to comfort me, like a security blanket. I can call my friends, but they've gotten tired of my anxiety attacks and they're not doing much better themselves. Some of them are in relationships, but they still binge on a lot of junk food."

Angela discovered that confidence comes *after* you focus on small, success-assured steps and *after* you gain a sense of mastery over your emotions and self-doubts. As she set small, intermediate goals that gave her positive feedback, she built confidence as she mastered increasingly more difficult steps. What I'd been saying all along finally made sense to her:

- Confidence and motivation are irrelevant to your executive decision to show up and do the job. You don't have to wait for your ego to feel confident, motivated, and all-knowing before your Strongest Self chooses to take action on achieving your goals.

- By performing the exercises in this book and applying the five qualities of your Strongest Self to your life, you've gained skills that improve your chances of moving beyond your ego's lack of confidence and of achieving your goals (for example, losing weight, stopping smoking, or writing a book).

Getting Started in Stage I: Realizing Goals, Intentions, and Dreams

When I introduced Angela to the four stages of effective change, she immediately saw why her prior attempts at change had been doomed to failure. They didn't start with changing her roles and perspective (the Awaken Your Strongest Self program), didn't give her time to ensure that every part of her was supporting her plan (Stage I), and didn't require that she prepare a plan for recovering from setbacks (Stage IV). They simply expected her to leap from her old habits to healthy habits, while operating from the same old ego perspective and limited coping skills.

I reminded Angela that in her new program, she was at Stage I (making up your mind), and that she had a few weeks to decide if she would commit to it. Her task now was to examine her reasons for making changes and the pros and cons of staying the same in her eating and exercise behavior. This was the time to build confidence that she could change and succeed at achieving her goals.

I asked Angela to make a contract with herself that she would not start making changes for at least two weeks. For now she would simply notice and record her initial thoughts and cravings in a journal (see Appendix A) whenever she binged or felt that some part of her wanted to binge. Like step 1 of the Awaken Your Strongest Self program, the first stage of the four stages of change starts with just noticing your initial responses and problematic patterns.

Your Awakened Self Has Extraordinary Tools

If you still experience a lack of confidence that you can achieve your goal, you're probably allowing a small ego part of you to be in charge of trying to make changes in your life. When your ego, or small you, is struggling to manage your life, it naturally feels overwhelmed and overburdened, and you can't trust it to overcome the obstacles you'll confront. Acting from a limited perspective, separate from your larger self, will make you vulnerable to using addictive habits to provide temporary relief from stress and upset. Without connection to a strong self to assert a vision, regulate your actions, stay congruent with your vision, and integrate all parts in the pursuit of your higher purpose, you are left with the lonely, arrogant struggle of your ego and what Buddhists call "the tyranny of your habitual mind."

From the perspective of your Strongest Self, however, Stage I of the effective change program involves holding a committee meeting (as you'll recall from Chapter 10) in which you address all the what ifs of those aspects that lack confidence and feel ambivalent. Though you've already demonstrated your interest in making positive changes in your life by starting the Awaken Your Strongest Self program, I strongly recommend that you still complete Stage I. This will ensure that you have answered all self-doubts and, therefore, can avoid possible self-sabotage of your goals by those parts that fear failure and are rebellious or critical. You then can be positive that every part of you is ready to commit to the entire journey of change and to embrace this new program of change.

Acting from your awakened Strongest Self, you have greater assurance that you can regulate your behavior to be congruent with your vision and goals. By applying the five qualities of your Strongest Self, you have healthy alternatives readily available to replace empty habits, outdated coping, and automatic reactions. Remember, you have five qualities to replace major blocks:

1. Safety replaces stress, worry, and anxiety.
2. Choice replaces ambivalence, indecisiveness, procrastination, and inner conflict.
3. Presence replaces the feeling of being overwhelmed.
4. Focus replaces self-criticism and self-blame.
5. Connection to the wisdom, compassion, and leadership of your Strongest Self replaces needless struggle and separateness.

In addition to the five qualities, you have powerful strategies, such as these:

- Getting a fear inoculation shot to motivate you to face fear
- Holding committee meetings to eliminate self-sabotage and gain cooperation
- Shifting to the perspective, roles, and voice of your Strongest Self and out of a limited sense of who you are and what you can do

Exercise for Stage I: Motivating Questions

Take a few minutes to quickly respond in your notebook to the following five questions. Return to them in the next few days to see what additions and changes you want to make.

1. What's the one thing you would change if you knew it would significantly improve the quality of your life?
2. What three qualities could you increase in your life in order to significantly improve your joy, inner peace, and satisfaction?
3. What three habits or patterns would you eliminate to significantly improve your self-satisfaction and self-esteem?
4. What are the top three questions or doubts you need to resolve before you're ready to commit to a program for achieving your goals and changing your habits?

5. What's one small action you'll perform *today* that could lead to a major improvement in your life and confidence?

In response to the last question, my clients have given the following answers (among others):

- Go to bed thirty minutes earlier.
- Unplug the TV.
- Drink a glass of water before every meal.
- Change into my exercise clothes as soon as I get home from work.
- Buy and slice up apples so they're ready as a snack.
- Spend five minutes doing nothing.
- Leave five minutes earlier for work or a meeting.

Take a week or two to notice your level of motivation to start a program for changing your habits and working toward achieving your goals. Answer any voices of ambivalence (what if . . . ?) and take your chairperson's seat at a committee meeting that unites all parts of you in support of your higher mission and goals. Then you'll be ready to move on to Stage II, committing to change.

12

Stage II

Committing to Change

Habits aren't flung out the window. They're coaxed down the stairs one step at a time.

—Mark Twain

IN THE FIRST STAGE of effective change, you considered the risks of staying the same and the pros and cons of committing to a new program for replacing destructive habits with healthy habits. Now it's time to shift from passively wishing to achieve your goal to actively committing to make it happen. At the completion of Stage I, you decided that there are psychological, physical, and emotional advantages to changing your habits and acquiring new, goal-achievement skills.

A major advantage of taking the time to complete Stage I is that you have the opportunity to build realistic expectations for how *you will make* this program work for you. You're not waiting for a magic wand that instantly dissolves weight or makes you not want to smoke a cigarette. You know from experience that no program will work for you unless you adjust it to your circumstances and personality. And you know there's no program that you cannot make work for you if you are determined to achieve your goal.

How to Prepare for Success in Stage II

In Stage II you're ready to declare your intention to make changes, experiment with making small changes, and set a date to take action. This is the time to make a clear, assertive statement: "I'm ready to set a specific date when I'll become a non-smoker, exercise almost every day, and add more vegetables to my meals to replace fattening foods." During this stage you prepare and experiment with healthy alternatives that replace your automatic reactions and address your underlying needs instead of just the conditioned wants of your lower brains.

Your wish—I want to lose twenty pounds, for example—states where you'd like to be in the future but says nothing about what you will do and when you will start on the path to getting there. Your wish or goal doesn't tell your mind and body how to maintain your commitment when you confront self-doubts, stressful events, distractions, and obstacles. Your body and brain need your effective leadership to assert a vision and a plan to make it a reality.

In this stage you experiment with small, success-assured steps—such as not eating after 9 P.M., working on your income taxes for fifteen minutes each day, or cutting back from two packs of cigarettes a day to one pack—and recording the thoughts and feelings (see Appendix A) that occur when you introduce these changes. Then, as in step 1 of the Awaken Your Strongest Self program, you identify the specific symptoms or cravings that tend to distract you from your commitments. *You cannot fail during this stage because you're simply gathering information.* Like an anthropologist from another galaxy, you're trying to understand what it takes for these earthlings to change unhealthy habits and to be effective in maximizing their potential.

It will be interesting to see the level of determination it takes to carry out a simple change in your usual pattern. After you've committed to a new path for your life, what will come to your mind and what might you feel compelled to do instead? If you decide to walk down the street without stopping, to what will your attention be drawn? Will your steps slow as you pass the window of a bakery, a shoe or clothing store, or a pizza and beer hangout? To walk toward your goal without hesitating requires a clear vision (which you prepared in Chapter 8), mental rehearsal (which you will complete in this chapter), a plan for taking action (which you will complete in Stage III in Chapter 13), and a plan to maintain your long-term success in spite of setbacks (which you will complete in Stage IV in Chapter 14).

Mental Rehearsal: A Plan for Overcoming Obstacles

Research on the stages of effective change reveals that plans or mental maps are an essential part of successfully negotiating the twists and turns of habit change. They work the way peak performance imagery works for athletes. In preparing for a major game or tournament, athletes include a mental rehearsal of what they'll do at each point and how they'll recover from losing a round, a set, or a quarter. Perhaps, most importantly, mental rehearsal involves building mental toughness to cope with both external and internal messages that say, "Give up, quit, you've lost." When you've achieved mental toughness you'll find that you're prepared to use such messages to rapidly shift your attention to your vision and what you can do now to optimize your chances.

To prepare for a week of experimenting with small changes in behaviors, you should do a mental rehearsal, as described in Chapter 1. In a mental rehearsal you identify your initial physical, emotional, and cognitive reactions that occur during the first two to five seconds. This will help you prepare for your default or knee-jerk reactions to any challenges that might arise. In a mental rehearsal you're the star of your own movie. You view your life from a distance, seeing and feeling yourself go through your day, watching for any upsetting events and reactions so you can choose to take actions that are congruent with your goals.

Mental rehearsals are best done with your eyes closed so you can see what occurs internally in your body, emotions, and imagery as life's challenges come across your path. When you use imagery to practice confronting a stressful situation or an upsetting emotion for thirty seconds without reverting to your usual escape mechanisms, you earn a fear inoculation shot that lessens your fear of future challenges. When you rehearse delaying your response for a few more breaths, you're offering your brain an alternative to reaching for your favorite comfort food or for your credit card as an attempt to get an instant fix and to escape uncomfortable feelings. You're communicating to your brain and body that you're strong enough to accept and contain more of life, that you're choosing to live a fuller life rather than continually run from fear or discomfort.

The mental rehearsal of your day may involve preparing for failed sales calls, overwhelming demands from your boss or customers, concerns about health issues, or another situation that triggers thoughts about escaping to some familiar habit. Zero in on the thoughts and feelings that precede your conditioned escape reaction, such as reaching for a cigarette, devouring another doughnut, or surfing the Internet.

Habits such as smoking, overeating, and procrastinating are merely attempted solutions for dealing with pain, loss, anxiety, and low self-esteem. They shouldn't be used as a reason for self-criticism. They're signs that you have an underlying need for self-acceptance that must be addressed to free yourself of dependency on these external fixes. As you awaken your higher brain and your Strongest Self to create plans and make choices, you're signaling that finally there's a mature self—someone stronger than your separated ego—that can manage your life, face your fears, and provide healthy ways of satisfying your needs.

Use Mental Maps to Chart Your Course

Mental maps help us identify the thoughts and feelings that precede our usual attempts to escape boredom, anxiety, loneliness, or agitation by seeking distractions and fixes. For example, in my case my favorite default reaction to feeling upset is to go to the local café for coffee and a pastry. Some part of me hopes to find there a nostalgic sense of gratification—regardless of how short-lived or how negative the long-term consequences—in a frustrating world.

I've become familiar with the words that run through my head—"I could use a cup of coffee and a muffin or a chocolate brownie"—and the sense of filling in time with eating and drinking rather than facing paperwork, an unpleasant telephone call, or a major project. I know that I'm most vulnerable to wanting a reward of some kind when I'm frustrated by computer problems or caught in phone menu hell that is supposed to offer customer service. There's a natural part of me that desperately wants to feel effective in a world that is largely beyond my control. It wants to be able to take action and seize a reward rather than feel powerless. Its cravings seem to say, "At least I can feed myself. I may not be able to control my government or my medical insurance, but I can buy something I want, gorge myself on sweets, and space out for a few hours."

I've practiced recognizing such thoughts as belonging to someone I feel compassion for, another human being who's vulnerable to the little irritants of modern life. But that's no longer me—it's only a former self that I no longer wholly identify with. Now I can shift more easily to a protective role toward my body and my life. This role empowers me to push aside most substances, habits, and fears that are toxic to my physical health, the full expression of my life, and the achievement of my goals. I also find it helpful to imagine that my innocent body and waistline are shouting, "Please, no more junk food. I'm already overloaded with years of unnecessary treats. Please don't take out your anger and frustration on me (again)."

There's certainly nothing wrong with taking a break and enjoying some guilt-free time at a café or indulging in your favorite ice cream or cake once in a while in moderation. It's only a problem when it becomes a habit that's diminished in its pleasure, because then it's anything but guilt-free. Then it becomes an *avoidance behavior*—a way of escaping something else —rather than a well-deserved and fully appreciated break. The vision I have for my life includes lots of high-quality guilt-free play, savoring food rather than gobbling, and an unambivalent commitment to my work. To sum up, it's my vision to live from my Strongest Self as much as I can. When you adopt a leader's perspective and protective role, you'll have a strong, magnetic vision to follow and you'll know when you've deviated from it.

Why Structure Works Better than Discipline. When I'm writing a book or preparing a seminar, I rely on behavioral structures to slow down my avoidant reactions and negative habits so I'm less likely to lose sight of my vision. One of the structures I use is unplugging the TV and taking the batteries out of the remote control. I can watch television, but now I must consciously *choose* to do it. With these self-imposed impediments in place, I now have time to decide on the best use of my time and if watching TV will offer me a legitimate, guilt-free break or just guilty procrastination. Having a structure in place that affords me a few more seconds to choose to face an important task doesn't feel like discipline to me.

For me, *discipline* implies an inner conflict among aspects of myself, with one part trying to control another part. As you learned earlier, making a higher brain choice can break inner conflict. Exercising executive-brain functions of choice, passion, and focus gains buy-in and cooperation from every part of me and is much more effective than discipline in achieving my goals. The time and effort involved in having to plug in the TV and find batteries for the remote gives my healthy alternatives (such as taking a walk, working on the next chapter, or paying my bills) a fair chance to compete with just simply pushing the remote control On button. This is not discipline; it's an act of humility that admits that I have little control over certain foods, events, places, and people. It's as if my ego is grounded in the *humus* (the earth) or in *humility* and acknowledges that it must rely on a higher and deeper wisdom to stay on the path if I'm going to achieve my full potential as an earthbound *human*.

The Peter Pans of this world attempt to fly above the earth, deny their humanness, and proclaim, "I'll never grow up. I'll never grow up." But my true self accepts the reality of its human limits and the consequences of its actions. That means I cannot bring pints of ice cream, chips, or certain cookies covered in dark chocolate into my house and fool myself that they will last more than twenty-four hours and that I'll achieve my health and fitness goals. When my separated ego is in charge, denial thrives and I fool myself into believing that I don't need to use behavioral structures or exercises to achieve my goals. Humility, however, is my Strongest Self's compassionate acceptance of the human condition, admiration for the courage of the human spirit, and gratitude for what I can accomplish when I connect with my deeper resources.

What behavioral structures or impediments will give you a little time to think and choose how to act when you're tempted to give in to a problematic habit? One client who wants to stop smoking has slowly moved her cigarettes farther and farther away from her desk. Others have increased their amount of walking by parking their car a few blocks away from the office and the store. Simple impediments such as wrapping cookies and treats in extra bags that require you to untie them before reaching in can slow down the frequency of overindulging on sweets.

Exercise: Making Mental Maps. Create an image in your mind of what a stressful day looks like for you, and imagine the typical challenges you face: frustration with traffic during your commute, an angry boss, dozens of urgent e-mails, computer problems, and troubling calls from your family. Plan what you'll say to yourself and what you'll do to stop yourself from reaching for your favorite distraction or sugary fix.

Use your mental map to chart your course through your day prepared for anything that could take you off the path to your goal. Your maps and plans will also prepare you with words, phrases, images, and reminders that help you to self-correct and strengthen your commitment to your vision. Use mental mapping every workday to ensure you're on target and awake to potential distractions that could take your attention away from your top priorities.

1. With your eyes closed, imagine that you are in a movie about one of your stressful days. Notice the events, feelings, thoughts, and people who distract you from your goals.

2. Identify the events that occur during a difficult day at work or school, such as being late or unprepared, and examine how they might cause you to revert to an unhealthy habit.

3. Identify the upsetting emotions that arise, such as feeling discouraged by a backlog of work, and how they might make you vulnerable to using distractions as an escape. Also, notice seemingly positive compulsions to suddenly vacuum, polish your shoes, or clean the grout in the shower. These urges are often warning signs that you're avoiding some task that you've defined as even more obnoxious.

4. Identify any worrisome thoughts, such as, "What if the boss doesn't like what I did on this project and I lose my job?" or "I can't stand this job and I can't do it any longer." Notice how hearing this internal voice might cause you to use one of your unhealthy escape mechanisms.

5. Prepare and use alternative thoughts, images, phrases, and actions that challenge and replace upsetting emotions, thoughts, and reactions to events. Use the five qualities you learned in Chapter 4, the focusing exercise in Chapter 8, and Angela's examples that follow.

Mental maps prepare you to identify your common distractions and to let them float down the stream of consciousness instead of pulling you into that cold stream when you attempt to grasp one of its intriguing thoughts. Distractions can then move through your awareness the way the sounds of traffic outside or planes overhead become background noise that no longer disturbs your focus. Your mental maps put your brain on alert for distracting thoughts about eating or smoking and habits such as constantly checking for e-mail and tell your brain that such distractions are outdated, empty habits that no longer deserve much attention. With practice you'll succeed in overriding your former default settings by replacing your initial thoughts and habitual responses with the five qualities of your Strongest Self that really satisfy your underlying needs and eliminate the compulsion to avoid your emotions or projects.

Angela: Testing Her Plan in Stage II

In Chapter 11 you found out that during Stage I, Angela spent two weeks just noticing how her fears of failure arose and subsided as she pondered the pros and cons of starting another program of change. She applied the Awaken Your Strongest Self strategy of not waiting for her ego to feel confident and motivated, which relieved her of worrying about her self-doubts and kept her focused on the small steps she could take to build confidence in her ability to make changes.

She began Stage II by taking on the role of an anthropologist who's researching how humans maintain and change their habits. This role allowed her to keep an observer's distance from her habitual responses and helped calm her self-critical and depressive feelings. She simply observed her initial reactions as interesting rituals and superstitions practiced by this strange species. In keeping with the guidelines for Stage II, Angela decided to experiment with stopping eating by 9 P.M., finding ways to add walking and stair climbing to her day, and fine-tuning her program for habit change. These pressure-free experiments helped her become aware of how frequently thoughts about food came to her mind, even when she wasn't hungry. She found that it helped to think of her food obsessions and cravings as simply empty, outdated habits that don't require her to frantically look for something to eat. She also discovered that it's easier to stop eating after dinner when she tells herself that she's fasting for twelve hours in preparation for a blood test at her doctor's office the next morning.

Even before Angela completed her two weeks in Stage II, she discovered that she wasn't always thinking about food and eating. This change encouraged her to believe that in the near future, as she said, "My life will not be about food. I won't have to think about it." She added this statement to her image of how her life will be when she reaches her goals. During this stage for experimentation and fine-tuning of her change program, Angela also practiced the Awaken Your Strongest Self tactic of waiting for a surprise from her subconscious mind and her deeper resources. This gave her the feeling of being connected to a wise part of her and of not having to tackle this overwhelming task alone. She practiced shifting from conscious mind worrying to wondering how she might play in the zone of peak performance. To get there her subconscious mind would have to work on how she'd fly over her ego's doubts and limited coping to transform her into a person who exercises regularly, protects her body from fattening foods, and uses food for nutrition rather than as a drug to control her emotions. Her subconscious-dreaming mind was now engaged in coming up with a creative solution.

Whenever familiar self-doubts arose, Angela would first tense her fists and hold her breath and then exhale and open her hands in a palms-up gesture while saying to herself:

- It's going to be interesting to see how I'll get through this day without binging.
- I wonder how I'll maintain my commitment to stop eating by 9 P.M.
- I'm expecting a surprise.

Moving from Worry to Wonder

Letting go of worry and opening up to wonder is another gesture of humility in which your ego lets go of struggling alone and discovers that it's connected to and supported by a deeper wisdom. The physical gesture of tightening your fists and furrowing your brow while you hold your breath simulates the tension of your worrying mind. You complete the process by exhaling, turning your palms up and opened, while shrugging your shoulders to indicate "It's out of my hands. I'm ready to receive a surprise."

When you practice switching from worry to wondering how your larger brain will help you achieve your goals and maintain your commitments, you might say:

- I wonder how I'll get through this day without losing my temper.
- It's going to be interesting to see how I maintain my commitment to inner peace.
- I wonder how I'll start on that project I've been avoiding. I haven't the foggiest idea how to do this, so it really will be interesting to watch myself start for fifteen minutes and go from not knowing to knowing.
- I wonder how I'll get through today without smoking a cigarette.
- It's going to be interesting to see how I will maintain my commitment to protect my body from toxic substances and habits.

These statements tell your subconscious mind to start working for you. They signal that your ego or limited sense of self is open to receiving support. Going from worry to wonder also acknowledges that your conscious mind cannot hold all the hours, months, and years required to complete a large and important task.

Every goal that is in the distant future—for example, losing forty-five pounds over the course of twelve months, finishing a book, completing college, or training for and running a marathon—must be back-timed into a present action so your body and mind know where and when to start. In the next exercise, you have the opportunity to imagine your future success and to connect it with the actions you can start today.

Exercise: Imagine Five Years Have Passed—Feel the Benefits of Change

Just as it's useful in Stage I to consider the pain of staying the same over the next five years, it's useful in Stage II to consider and imagine how much better your life can be when you start a process of change. Imagine that five years have passed since you've completed the Awaken Your Strongest Self program, and many marvelous, unimagined positive changes have occurred. Say to yourself, "It's the year 20___, I'm ___ years old, and five years ago I started to make major changes in my perspective, in my sense of who I am, and in my life. Tonight, to celebrate my accomplishments I'm having a party with my friends, and I want to tell them of my journey." See yourself in your ideal home with new and old friends, and think about the following:

1. Consider how you started five years ago and the initial steps you took that led to major, transformative changes. Tell your friends about how you expanded your sense of self, made changes in how you act, and now can adopt new roles that enable you to effectively manage and guide your life.

2. Looking back from five years in the future, consider the obstacles you've had to overcome and the fears you've faced. Appreciate what you've learned and the changes you've made to reach your ideal level of physical health, financial success and security, and happiness in your relationships. Express your gratitude for attaining inner peace and self-contentment and for the old and new friendships that supported your growth and your perseverance on your path. Write out what you tell your friends about your journey over the last five years.

Your Brain Is Waiting for Your Decision

Your decision to start working on a life-changing project communicates to your lower fight-or-flight brain, "I'm not running away. I'm determined to problem solve, and I'm expecting creative solutions from my right brain and subconscious mind." Your brain responds with creative solutions within a few breaths, as if to say, "If you're that determined to override primitive fears, I'll have to shift from the stress response drive of your mental computer to the problem-solving drive. I'll get back to you with some creative solutions in about ten to twenty seconds."

Starting a project or a process of change is like climbing a mountain trail. Your muscles warm up, your breathing adapts to the altitude, and you gain a better perspective and new information once you get going. You build physical strength and endurance, and each new vista and discovery activates your curiosity and motivation. The climb may be difficult at first, but it becomes easier as your body adapts, and you feel good that you continued through the tough parts to make it to the top, where you're rewarded with a spectacular vista. And you discover that you can do more than you thought you could.

A part of you may still remember and feel bad about reverting to self-destructive behaviors in the past, such as binging on cookies or television or compulsively phoning ex-partners. But you'll gradually build self-respect and confidence as you get through the first few days and weeks without caving in to these primitive ways of coping. You'll begin to understand that some nervousness and anxiety are natural and manageable when you start a daunting task or take the initial steps up the path to your goal.

Exercise: The Strength of Your Intentions

Before you move on to Stage III: Taking Action, rate the strength of your intentions to ensure that you're ready to commit to a program of effective change and succeed. If you feel unable to make a commitment at this time, reread Chapters 10 and 11 and remember that it's your Strongest Self that makes the intention to change, not your ego. Write three intentions, and use the following scales to see how prepared you are to move forward on one or two or all three. Here are a few examples:

- I intend to walk thirty minutes a day, six days a week.
- I intend to eat three to five servings of fruits and vegetables each day.
- I intend to start writing the next chapter of my book for at least thirty minutes every day.

1. I intend to make changes in my life, my habits, and my sense of self within the next two weeks.

ABSOLUTELY NOT TRUE	NOT TRUE	MODERATELY TRUE	TRUE	ABSOLUTELY TRUE
1	2	3	4	5

2. I know when, where, what, and how I'll start making changes in my life and on my habits.

ABSOLUTELY NOT TRUE	NOT TRUE	MODERATELY TRUE	TRUE	ABSOLUTELY TRUE
1	2	3	4	5

3. I am making a commitment to start within the next two weeks on a specific step, at a specific time. (Write the date and time you'll start taking action on your new, healthy habit.)

ABSOLUTELY NOT TRUE	NOT TRUE	MODERATELY TRUE	TRUE	ABSOLUTELY TRUE
1	2	3	4	5

4. I have a plan to deal with distractions, loss of confidence, and lack of motivation. I have a clear vision that I will use every day to act like a magnet that keeps me on the path to my goals.

ABSOLUTELY NOT TRUE	NOT TRUE	MODERATELY TRUE	TRUE	ABSOLUTELY TRUE
1	2	3	4	5

SCORING

16–20 Take one to two weeks to experiment with small changes in your behavior, and you'll be ready for the next chapter, on Stage III, taking action.

12–15 Before you go on to Stage III, review the exercise in Chapter 11 ("Imagine Five Years Have Passed—Feel the Pain of Staying the Same") in which you consider the negative consequences of not changing. And use Angela's "Questions to Help You Build Confidence and Self-Esteem," also in Chapter 11, to slowly strengthen your belief in your ability to make changes.

4–11 You could benefit from rereading Chapters 10 and 11. You may need the help of a coach, counselor, or support group to cope with your ambivalence about making positive changes and to learn what it takes to overcome ingrained habits.

There's no need to keep your brain and body waiting any longer for a higher brain decision to pursue your dreams. If you've completed the exercises in this and the previous chapter—and scored above 15 on the preceding exercise—you're adequately prepared to set a date to launch your new commitment to optimize your potential. A deeper confidence will come *after* you start.

13

Stage III

Taking Action

*[A]sk the question: Does this path have a heart? . . . A path with-
out a heart is never enjoyable. . . . On the other hand, a path with
a heart is easy; it does not make you work at liking it.*

> —Carlos Castaneda, *The Teachings of Don Juan: A Yaqui Way
> of Knowledge*

WELCOME TO STAGE III, taking action, where indecision, lack of
confidence, passively wishing for the goal, and making excuses
have no place. In this stage you get to flex your leadership muscles and keep your inner team focused on what to do. Your full
attention is on your path in the present while your future goals
and magnetic vision are pulling you forward step by step and day
by day.

   If you were in a movie, the director would be shouting,
"Action!" Rehearsals and experimentation are in the past. This
is it—the day you start on the path to eliminating the old and
bringing in your new habits. This is the day you throw out all
your cigarettes, give away the ice cream in the freezer, buy fruit
and vegetables, and put your running shoes on as soon as you get

home from work. You're on the path, and at this stage the path is more important than your goal.

Choosing a Path with a Heart During Stage III

Carlos Castaneda's medicine man, Don Juan, tells us that the goal is almost irrelevant. He says that when you reach your goal, you'll find that it leads to another path. So choose a path that has a heart, embrace it completely, and experience the "great peace and pleasure [of] traversing its length." His words poetically communicate the wisdom that the end does not justify the means—that it's not the destination but the journey that counts. So choose a path not because it leads to your goal but because the path itself brings you in line with your true self and forges all parts of you into a powerful, integrated team. On this journey each step toward your goal, each small success, builds momentum and makes it increasingly easier to deflect distractions and to align your actions with your higher vision.

You may find that of all the stages of change, Stage III is the easiest because you've made up your mind about your commitment and you've clarified your vision. You're working in the present, with a purpose, focused on what you'll do each day to advance closer to your goal. However, you still need to anticipate distractions and some initial stiffness as you move from passive wishing to active engagement on your path to your goals.

Barriers to Taking Action: Inertia and Fear

Initially, change of any kind can be difficult because you're facing the law of physics that says a body at rest tends to remain at rest and a body in motion tends to stay in motion. Staying at rest is comfortable but can be dangerous to your health and long-term happiness. To advance in life we must go through the uncomfortable first steps of overcoming inertia before we can experience the excitement and ease of momentum. We must shift through the lower gears of the engine before we reach an efficient cruising speed.

The path to changing habits and introducing new life habits is no different. We must be prepared for some discomfort during the first few minutes, days, and weeks. We need a clear vision, a plan that specifies what actions to take, and a plan that tells us how to return to our path when we've veered off course.

Aside from inertia, the other main barriers to taking action and making changes in our lives involve a variety of fears: fear of failure; fear of success; fear of criticism, embarrassment, and shame; and fear of self-hatred and self-punishment. These fears are often expressed like this: "What if I fail (again)? What if they don't like my work? What if I make myself miserable?" It's this voice that could keep you from starting today on the path that leads to a healthier, fuller, and more satisfying life. But this voice is simply doing its job of reminding you of the need for a survival plan to cope with situations you've labeled as dangerous. This voice also needs an updated method to replace the ineffective, default ways of coping that keep you stuck in procrastination and other destructive habits. The what ifs of your worrying mind are asking you to awaken your Strongest Self to provide compassionate acceptance, guidance toward your vision, and a plan for taking action.

Creating Action Plans

Action plans—in which you write down when, where, and how you will perform a goal behavior—help people increase the frequency of healthy habits, such as exercise. Research on enhancing the motivation to exercise, reported in the *British Journal of Health Psychology*, found that the more elaborate the mental simulation of the action steps, "the higher is the probability to initiate the intended behavior." That is, having a mental rehearsal (creating pictures in your mind) of what you intend to do and specifying when, where, and how you'll do it increase the odds that you'll start on the actions that lead to your goals. This finding applies whether your goal is to exercise more, eat healthier foods, stop smoking, or work consistently on top-priority projects.

Exercise: Strengthen Your Action Plans with Questions

Project into the future a few months and imagine that your worrying mind and "what if" voice have become nicely behaved assistants to your Strongest Self. Instead of plaguing you with guilt and shouting their concerns, they simply and quietly ask the following questions to strengthen your mental maps and clarify how to make your goals a reality:

1. When do you want to start working on your goals? List the day and time.

2. Where will you start? See the place and time clearly, and make note of any distractions you need to remove from this place.

3. What will you start on? Buying vegetables for dinner? Taking a thirty-minute walk before dinner? Last year's income taxes?

4. How will you perform your goal behavior? Will you go to the gym? Will you start writing at the library or neighborhood café? Will you start dinner with a salad and extra vegetables?

5. How will you remind yourself to focus on your goals when you are about to make choices? How will you remember to buy fruits and vegetables and keep from buying fattening foods? How will you remember to exercise?

6. How will you keep to your commitments? To your commitment of not eating after dinner or 9 P.M.? To your commitment to exercise your body when you're traveling or working ten-hour days?

Creating Behavioral Goal Statements

An action plan gives you a clear action step that can be summarized by a question you need to repeat throughout your day: "When can I start on my goal?" Clients who have worked with me on overcoming procrastination post that question all over their office and home. This question prompts them to choose a time and place: "I will start at 8 A.M. at my computer for thirty minutes." Their clear answer demonstrates effective leadership and tells their body and mind specifically when and where to show up and start. It replaces the old default of thinking, "I have to finish a big project that I'd rather not do," which, of course, evokes procrastination rather than motivation.

To make your goal tangible, state it in clear, behavioral language that can be measured. You should know when you're performing your goal behavior and when you've achieved your goal. Write down a measurable goal, a deadline, and the action you will take every day to achieve it.

Examples of goal statements include the following:

Goal: I will lose twenty pounds.
Deadline: In six months.
Daily Action: By eating more fruits and vegetables instead of candy and cookies or by reducing my caloric intake by 500 calories a day (which equals 3,500 calories per week, or one pound) and going to the gym three times a week.

Goal: I will lower my blood pressure.
Deadline: In three months.
Daily Action: By walking six days a week for thirty minutes at a time or by doing aerobic exercise at the gym for forty-five minutes three times a week.

Goal: I will complete a draft of four to six chapters for my book.
Deadline: In six months.
Daily Action: By working fifteen hours per week—approximately one hour a day during the week and ten hours on the weekend. (*Note:* while finding fifteen hours in your week may seem impossible, keep in mind that the average American watches more than thirty hours of television per week; many seemingly overwhelming goals can be achieved by investing fifteen hours per week.)

Now write out the three parts of your own behavioral goal statement:

Goal: _____
Deadline: _____
Daily Action: _____

_____

Exercise: Priming Your Brain for Success

Having a clear behavioral goal statement greatly improves the probability that you will be able to get started on the specific actions necessary to make progress. But this additional exercise satisfies your need for emotional connections that support you on the path toward your goal. As you show up each day to fulfill your commitments, it's nice to know that you're not doing this alone. This exercise connects you to your past and future selves and the compassion and wisdom of your Strongest Self, making the journey so much more joyful.

Imagine that you're in a comfortable theater with a movie screen divided into three parts. Use three breaths in three parts—inhale, hold your breath and tighten your muscles, and then exhale—to float down into your chair in the theater. Use this diagram (Figure 13.1) to help you visualize the three-part movie screen. As the house lights dim in the theater, a light illuminates the left panel of the screen in a color that represents you in your current state.

1. See yourself in the present. See yourself from head to toe as you look and feel now on the left side of the movie screen. Communicate nonverbally to that person on the screen that, even though he or she can't see you, you're out there providing compassion and understanding. You know better than anyone else what this person has been through and the dreams and goals he or she is hoping to achieve. Let this person know that regardless of current issues and past failures, you accept him or her completely. Write down what you'd like to communicate to your present self.

FIGURE 13.1 Priming Your Brain for Success

1. Present	3. Transition from Present to Future	2. Future Ideal
See yourself as you look and feel now.	*See and feel yourself in transition from your present to your ideal future self.*	*See and feel yourself happy, healthy, joyful, fulfilled, and successful.*

Take a moment to temporarily say good-bye to this part of you, knowing that you will stay connected to each other and that you can always return. As the light dims on the far left panel of the screen, a new color, which represents you in your future, ideal state, illuminates the far right panel.

2. See your future, ideal self. Imagine yourself happy, healthy, joyful, fulfilled, and successful. See yourself as you will look and feel a few months or a year from now. Communicate nonverbally to that person on the screen that you are there supporting him or her with compassion and understanding and celebrating in his or her success. After all, you know better than anyone else what this person has been through to reach this point in life. Let this person know that you accept him or her completely. Write down what you'd like to communicate to your future, ideal self.

Take a moment to temporarily say good-bye to this part of you, knowing that you will stay connected to each other and that you can always return. As the light dims on the far right panel of the screen, another new color, which represents you in transition, on the path to successful change (Stage III), illuminates the middle panel.

3. Imagine yourself in transition from your present to your future, ideal self. See yourself as you look and feel on the daily path of commitment to your new, healthy habits. Communicate nonverbally to that person on the screen that you are supporting him or her with compassion and understanding. After all, you know better than anyone else the challenges this person faces each day on the path. Let him or her know that this isn't a solo journey. Let this person know that you've seen the end of this movie and you know he or she is going to make it. This person simply needs to face one day at a time, filling in the steps that lead to a fulfilled, joyful self. Write down what you'd like to communicate to the part of you that is in transition.

Take a moment to temporarily say good-bye to this part of you, knowing that you will stay connected to each other and that you can always return. As the light dims on the center panel of the screen, the house lights come up slowly.

4. You find yourself comfortably centered in your chair, supported by your past and your future and aligned with yourself in transition. You've been acting in the protective and leadership roles of your Strongest Self and from its higher perspective and deeper wisdom. How will you bring these roles and perspectives into your everyday life as you begin the journey toward a life in which your vision, goals, and action are congruent with who you wish to be?

Taking Charge of Your Habits

Parents with teenagers are often amazed at how motivated their children become about their studies when they must achieve higher grades to earn the right to drive the family car. This tangible and definite goal, even though months away, can stimulate focus and motivation on tasks that were previously ignored. Even more remarkable is the mental toughness of students who want to work in fields such as medicine that require years of education and training. Their rewards—the completed training, prestige, and income—are typically ten to fifteen years in the future. In the meanwhile, students must face the discomfort of studying math, biology, and chemistry while missing out on having fun with their friends.

People pursuing a distant goal must ensure that they're not creating the habit of quitting by rewarding it with TV or snacking. To make persistence a habit, they still give themselves rewards, but only after doing fifteen to thirty minutes of facing something difficult. Those who comfortably persevere on long-term goals give themselves a sense of accomplishment whenever they take another step toward their desired objective. They're generous self-leaders who reinforce progress rather than punish errors. And they're able to realistically picture themselves in the roles they will play ten to fifteen years in the future. They can taste it, see it, and feel it. They make the results of the goal real for them now. They live as if they've already achieved the goal, and they feel like the professional they're about to become.

The Rewards of Persistence

I've worked with clients who want to lower their blood pressure and lose weight but who haven't walked or jogged for more than five minutes in twenty years because "it's too hard and I feel too tired at the end of the day." I tell them it takes at least six minutes for your muscle fibers to warm up and another six to fourteen minutes before you start burning fat. After your initial six to twenty minutes of walking at a good pace, it becomes easier. Because fat contains nine calories per gram, as opposed to four for protein and carbohydrates, once you burn fat—after about twelve to twenty minutes of movement—you get a rush of energy called a second wind or a runner's high. Another reason to get past the first six minutes of inertia is that working your leg muscles helps return blood to your heart so it doesn't have to work so hard. This principle of giving yourself time to warm up applies to other goal behaviors, such as writing and studying for exams. It includes the quality of connection to the wisdom of your mind and body and the principle of expecting a surprise.

Once you give your mind a blueprint of what you want to achieve or solve, it starts looking for clues that fill in the steps or the pieces of the puzzle. Each chapter of this book started with an outline (or blueprint) of the main concepts and was filled in with examples that came to me while I was going about my life doing something else. When you give your mind a blueprint of what you want to build in your life, your brain begins to warm up its circuitry to look for the necessary material to complete the job. You don't complete overwhelming tasks such as writing a book or losing forty-five pounds with your ego struggling alone but with the cooperation of many parts of your brain and psyche.

Angela: Taking Baby Steps to Treat Despair in Stage III

When Angela started Stage III, she'd already taken a month to use the Awaken Your Strongest Self program to help her develop new ways of coping with stress, anxiety, and loneliness. During that initial month of learning to shift her perspective—and the additional month she took to move through the first two stages of effective change—Angela went from hopelessness, low motivation, and low self-esteem to really believing in herself and her ability to make significant changes in her life. She now was ready to work on the thoughts, attitudes, and behaviors that would help her stop binging, increase her exercise, and lose weight.

Within the first thirty days of starting on Stage III, Angela lost five pounds even though she wasn't officially dieting and didn't feel deprived. Her experiments during Stage II showed Angela that she could stop eating by 9 P.M., find times when she could walk for ten to twenty minutes on errands rather than taking the car, and enjoy going to the gym three times a week. She found that the tactics she'd learned in other programs—such as recording what she ate, drinking water before each meal, and brushing and flossing after each meal—also helped her reduce her tendency to unconsciously overeat. The difference was that this time, all the strategies and tactics fit together as part of her new ability to identify her habitual, default responses to stress and upset and to replace them with healthy habits.

At times Angela had a hard time getting out of bed in the morning. I reminded her that she had learned a major skill from the Awaken Your Strongest Self process: focus on what you can do rather than on what is out of your control. Switch from thoughts about the goal, which is in the future and is usually overwhelming, to thoughts about what you can do in the present.

Controlling Habits Lowers Stress and Suffering

One behavioral tactic for dealing with despair is to take very small steps. If you're finding it difficult to get out of bed in the morning, don't think, "I have to lose forty-five pounds" or "I have to complete thirty things on my to-do list." Just aim for wiggling your toes and pulling the covers back. If you succeed at that, try putting your feet on the floor and standing up. Once you've accomplished that, take a few steps to the bathroom and reward yourself with a hot shower. Notice and push aside any thoughts about going back to bed. Then think about breakfast and getting dressed. Even if you don't feel like going to work, get yourself out of the house and walk around the block. As your body comes alive when moving and breathing more fully, chances are you will feel better and can make a better decision about what to do next.

Focus on what you can do, and reward yourself for all steps you take in the right direction. Find ways to say, "Good, I got started." Show compassion for the part of you that feels sad, and appreciate what you are achieving. The same principle applies to business. If you're in sales, define success as making the calls, not on closing the sale. Once you've broken through your resistance to making calls, you can work on improving your percentage of closed sales. If you're a student or a writer, focus on when you can start for thirty minutes on your project rather than on the overwhelming image of completing a two-hundred-page manuscript.

The emotional component of dealing with despair can be more complex and often requires psychotherapy, but you can start with self-acceptance as a replacement for self-criticism. Effective leaders, and effective self-leaders, know how to reward all steps in the right direction at a ratio of four statements of praise to one "needs improvement." When you identify what you're doing right, you're giving your brain a picture of what actions it should repeat. Criticism can cause confusion because it's punishing without indicating what to do. As Ken Blanchard says in *The One Minute Manager*, "Catch them doing something right."

Catch Yourself Doing Something Right

While you're taking action on the path to your goals, a bit of self-criticism might arise about how you should've stopped smoking earlier, started working on three years of back taxes sooner, or begun an exercise program years ago when you were younger. You can tell your critical dictator, "Stop it! I'm doing what I can to change things. I'm taking action now. I'm making progress. And in spite of my imperfections, I accept my current situation and myself as I am and where I am."

Listening to every part of yourself and offering acceptance addresses your underlying needs and thereby helps eliminate most cravings for junk food and junk solutions. Your self-acceptance and the tools you've been learning to use have given you new ways to cope with stress, loss, and disappointment. Don't be surprised if accepting yourself and your situation slows down some of your compulsive behaviors to the point where you don't feel the need to reach for a cigarette or a cookie or to escape difficult tasks.

Sometime in the next twenty-four hours, you'll brush your teeth—you might even floss. With the support of your subconscious mind and your body, you'll perform dozens of healthy habits without having to think about them as being difficult or burdensome. You've made them automatic, healthy default patterns. It can be the same with your bigger, and seemingly more difficult, goals. You're on the path to making your goal behaviors a daily procedure that can become automatic. In the next chapter you'll complete the four-stage program of effective change by preparing to recover from setbacks and maintain your progress.

14

Stage IV

Maintaining Long-Term Success

What is needed . . . is self-efficacy to cope with barriers that make the intended action so difficult. Self-efficacious individuals imagine success scenarios where they make fruitful attempts and pass through different courses of action that lead to positive outcomes . . . they see more options and invent more strategies.

—Ralf Schwarzer, "Thought Control of Action: Interfering Self-Doubts," in *Cognitive Interference*

LET'S IMAGINE that the concepts and exercises you've learned in this book have stirred your motivation to improve your life and taken you through the first thirty days of positive habit change. You've learned how to catch your old patterns within minutes and replace them with healthy, effective alternatives. You've gained freedom from old fears and destructive patterns and taken steps to turn your dreams into reality. You are beginning to feel comfortable with exercising more frequently, focusing on top-priority projects every day, eating healthy foods, and living from the perspective of your Strongest Self.

As you continue to exercise your executive-brain functions, you feel more in control of the direction of your life and are less distracted from your path and commitments. You justifiably feel empowered, effective, and confident that you can make transformative changes in your life. But there may be a nagging worry in the back of your mind, and you may ask yourself, "Yes, but what will I do if thirty days from now I have a couple of bad days and backslide into my old habits?" Answering that question is what Stage IV is all about. In this final stage of change, you'll learn exercises to help you maintain your new skills even if you experience a temporary lapse into archaic survival patterns. You'll learn how to recover from setbacks and how to strengthen your ability to shift to the larger identity of your awakened Strongest Self. Remember, lapses don't signal the end of the game for you. Rather, they signal that you've had a short success and that now it's time to get back to the basics and use the tools, examples, and exercises that can work for you to create long-term success.

Bouncing Back from Setbacks: The Key to Stage IV

You don't need to be a fortune-teller to predict that within thirty to ninety days something will occur that could throw you back to using old habits as a source of temporary comfort. That something might be lightning frying your computer; a financial loss; an unpleasant interaction with a customer, coworker, or loved one; or a party that includes lots of drinks, sweets, and smoking. In fact, the research shows that most people have a setback in their weight loss and smoking cessation commitments between day thirty and day ninety. It's essential, therefore, to have plans for coping with lapses if you want to maintain an effective program of habit change for the long term.

Exercise: Mark Your Calendar

This would be a good time to mark your calendar with the dates of your thirty-, sixty-, and ninety-day anniversaries of starting to take action on your goal and to record your successful days on your path. You may want to include a note on each of those anniversaries that says, "Reawaken My Strongest Self." These anniversary dates can remind you to get back to the basics of three-part breathing and applying the five qualities of your Strongest Self to lower your anxiety, bring your mind into the present, and connect with your larger support system. On these dates check to make sure that you haven't slipped into making your goal a should or a have to with which you passively comply and then resist. Remember that in Stages I and II you considered the pros and cons of making changes and fully *choosing* to take small steps toward transformation. With each anniversary reawaken your higher brain functions to proactively *rechoose* and *recommit* to your goal.

Make copies of Appendix E to record your goal, the action you intend to take, when you'll start, any obstacles or distractions you experience, and your healthy alternatives.

Don't Let Setbacks Stop Your Progress

Experiencing minor lapses—such as smoking one or two cigarettes, eating one bag of cookies, or procrastinating one day on a major project—isn't a reason to give up on your commitments. In Stage IV you practice keeping your eyes on the prize regardless of slips, setbacks, mistakes, and disappointments. You're planning for long-term maintenance of your habit change program.

If you were to apply this program to stop smoking, you'd need to know what to do if you lapsed by smoking one or more cigarettes. You'd have to prepare yourself to deflect the impulse to give up and jettison all the progress you'd made in the last thirty to sixty days. Part of your plan to stay resilient would be to throw away any remaining cigarettes and recommit to protecting your body and life from tobacco. On your calendar you'd mark and number every successful day as a nonsmoker (or in the case of other habits, as a daily athlete, of not binging, and so on), skip any day on which you lapse, and continue counting the next day as your thirty-first or sixty-first day on the path to your goal. Take credit for all *short successes.*

A forty-one-year-old carpenter named Jim told me, "I left our first session feeling wonderful and hopeful. I thought to myself, I'm going to finally quit smoking. Within twenty-four hours, I had several very stressful events from my family and from work. I drove to the emergency room to see my father, worrying all the way and smoking cigarette after cigarette. I failed again." Prior smoking cessation programs Jim tried had not prepared him to deal with such lapses. He considered himself a failure and was ready to give up once again. In fact, from the larger perspective of long-term maintenance of healthy habits, his lapse was an opportunity to learn how to strengthen his plan. Jim needed to prepare for such stressful events and be ready with coping statements and actions so he could rapidly recover and get back on track.

Angela: Overcoming Setbacks in Stage IV

During her first thirty days of taking action on her goals, Angela made considerable progress. But as she approached her sixtieth day, she began to forget to use the tools that helped her to increase her exercise routine, lessen her use of food as a drug, and lose eleven pounds in two months. In spite of her successes, feeling stressed led her to lapse into binging on two occasions.

Binging was the most difficult habit for Angela to control. It seemed to arise automatically when she had a stressful day or when she started feeling that she had to do so many things for other people, particularly her demanding bosses and her family. On such days some part of her just wanted a treat for all the distress she'd endured as well as for having to suppress her true feelings. This part of her would act out its unfulfilled needs with a voice that said, "I deserve a break. I suffered and need something to unwind." It doesn't take much of a leap to go from this attitude to drinking, smoking, and zoning out in front of the tube while mindlessly gobbling thousands of extra calories.

As with many habits that seem to erupt unexpectedly, such as pro-crastination and smoking, binge eating tends to be worse in the evening after a day of stress. If you've had to put up with a demeaning, unfulfill-ing work situation all day, some part of you wants to rebel against the dictator who's been beating you up with to-do lists and have tos.

Angela's binging is an example of how we often use a destructive habit in an attempt to solve deeper problems from our ego's limited per-spective and limited coping skills. The basic problem to be resolved is often one of inner conflict and feeling separated from your larger, wiser self. As you begin to live from the third perspective of choice, you elim-inate much of the inner conflict between the voices of "you have to" ver-sus "I don't want to." You tap into your Strongest Self's ability to speak up and stand up for your rights and your needs. For Angela it was essen-tial to do Chapter 13's "Priming Your Brain for Success" exercise daily so that she felt connected to her ideal self and was able to give herself messages of acceptance, forgiveness, and compassion as she faced the day-to-day challenges of staying on her path.

Angela found that when she lowered her daytime stress by being more assertive at work and less available to play rescuer for her family, she did, in fact, lessen her compulsion to binge in the evening. Her renewed commitment to herself included going to the gym after work to give her a healthy treat of one to two hours away from the demands of her job and her family. This healthy break fed the part of her that felt deprived and made her feel more powerful in protecting her health and her life. It also lessened her need to rebel in ways that were destructive to her health and the achievement of her long-term goals.

Self-Sabotage and Your Ego

Have you ever noticed how once you start being successful and achieving your dream, some people want to rain on your parade? They may accuse you of changing, as if that were a major crime. Even your own ego gets jealous of how much happier you are now that it's no longer running your life. Lapses sometimes mean that your ego is trying to resume command of your life. By nature the ego believes it's separate from the rest of the brain, body, and universe. In its arrogance and insistence on struggling alone, it refuses to acknowledge its dependence on outside help and considers such help a crutch.

When your higher self uses an integrated team effort that makes things easier, the ego tends to feel unemployed and is waiting to say, "See, I told you it wouldn't work. You need me to struggle for you. I knew anything that easy wouldn't work. I'd rather be right than happy." The ego would rather use its drugs to sustain its lonely struggle than accept the fact that you can achieve greater ease, joy, and success by integrating your various resources under the leadership of your Strongest Self.

What's most remarkable is that once your ego discovers that the self is truly present and willing to take responsibility for managing your life, it will begin to cooperate. Even its worrying mind will begin to soften its what ifs and will show up to watch for the surprise as it experiences how rapidly and easily you recover from upset and distractions when you're connected to a larger, wiser, and stronger support system. Eventually, your ego will learn to actually enjoy working more creatively as part of a team that includes the wisdom of your subconscious mind and the leadership of your Strongest Self.

When you use your higher brain functions of integration, choice, and commitment, you demonstrate your leadership skills and eliminate the doubts and ambivalence that lead to self-sabotage. Once you start responding to your ego's fears of failure by providing coping plans, you'll further establish yourself as an able leader who deserves cooperation rather than resistance.

How Coping Plans Can Remove Distractions

Combining your action plans from the last chapter with *coping plans*—which specify how you'll cope when obstacles arise—increases the likelihood that you'll start and maintain your goal activities. Both action and coping plans involve the use of your brain's prefrontal cortex executive functions and, therefore, put your higher self in charge of lower and more primitive brain reactions. Coping plans work to automatically manage distractions that occur during performance of your goal behaviors. In fact, your rehearsal of anticipated obstacles, challenges, and opportunities forms new neural pathways in your brain to challenge your default reactions and bring you to a new destination.

Coping plans are similar to preparations for a natural disaster or a camping trip. You want to make sure you have the essential items (such as water, portable radios, flashlights, and food) to last through the first days of a disaster as well as a plan for connecting with family and friends. I would add that you also need a mental rehearsal so you know what your initial, default reactions—for example, fear, pain, or self-criticism—might be and how to shift to actions that are more compatible with survival.

Exercise: Making Your Coping Plans

Coping plans involve identifying potential barriers and distractions to achieving your goal and preparing ways of overcoming them.

1. Write three barriers or distractions that could keep you from performing a healthy behavior or cause you to engage in a destructive one. You can use the barriers you identified in the last chapter. Ask yourself this question: "What could cause me to _____ [insert a possible destructive behavior]?" (Barrier #1. Barrier #2. Barrier #3.)

- **Example 1:** What could cause me to not exercise? (I had to work late. It's raining. I'm too busy.)
- **Example 2:** What could cause me to overeat? (I'm bored. I got an upsetting call. I need to treat myself.)
- **Example 3:** What could cause me to smoke? (I'm anxious. I hate to wait without doing something. I need to stay awake.)

- **Example 4:** What could cause me to procrastinate? (I feel overwhelmed. I don't like this part of the job. I don't know what to write.)

2. Write down what will you say and do to keep to your commitment to your goal in spite of these obstacles. Your coping plan links distracting events or feelings to a phrase and a planned action that keeps you focused on your goal behavior. Coping plans have this basic structure: "When _____ [potential distraction] occurs, I will say _____ [inner dialogue] and I will do _____ [corrective action]."

- **Example 1:** When I become overwhelmed and think about eating, smoking, or surfing the Internet, I will say, "Focus," and then take three deep breaths and choose one task to start on for fifteen to thirty minutes.
- **Example 2:** When I feel depressed and worthless, I will say, "Yes, this feels awful, but it's not the end of the world." I will start working on one simple task, take a walk, or call a friend.
- **Example 3:** When my mind makes excuses to not exercise, I will say, "Yes, those are the usual excuses. I'm just going to the gym without arguing." I will stop what I'm doing and dress for the gym or a walk.

3. You can strengthen the effectiveness of your coping plans when you apply what you've learned from the Awaken Your Strongest Self steps. When you notice a distracting thought, craving, or feeling, you can do the following:

- Identify it as a small part of you—not your whole self.
- Speak to that part in the compassionate voice of the self that says, "Yes . . . and your worth is safe. Regardless of

what happens, I won't make you feel bad. You're not alone with this task and feeling. I'll choose what to do."

- Use the self's qualities of safety, choice, presence, focus, and connection to replace the symptoms of stress, inner conflict, feeling overwhelmed, self-criticism, and struggling alone.

Example: When I identify that part that says, "I'm too busy to take a walk," I'll say, "Yes, I'm busy, and that's why I need to walk, so I can feel refreshed and do my job more efficiently and creatively—working smarter, not harder." Then I'll get up from my chair, desk, or computer immediately to walk, or I'll set a time when I can walk later today. I'll enjoy thinking about how good I'll feel tomorrow when I discover that I've chosen to start on the project I've been avoiding for so long. I'll feel connected to a larger team as a member who's run his or her part of a relay race so the next lap is easier for my future self. Tomorrow I'll be grateful that I started on this yesterday, making it easier for myself today. It's as if I have a personal assistant who's set things up so I can get right to work on what's most important.

Creating Coping Statements

As part of her tool kit for overcoming distractions from her goals, Angela and I constructed seven statements she could read and recite whenever she was tempted to revert to her old habits of overeating. We put together seven more statements to help her maintain her commitment to physical activity. You can adapt and apply these examples to maintaining your own healthy habits by building your distraction-challenging statements.

- I can eat slowly, feel satisfied sooner, and stop eating before I feel stuffed.

- I've had plenty; I don't need much. I can choose when to have a dessert in the future. There's plenty to eat. I won't starve.
- I can always have water, fruit, and vegetables. I can enjoy an apple and find that I feel full and satisfied.
- I've enjoyed my day and given myself healthy breaks. I don't need another break today that involves fattening, processed food.
- My body has inherited the ability to store extra calories as fat in case of famine and long journeys without food. My body is safe from famine. I have plenty of extra food. I won't starve.
- I can stay with feelings of hunger until my next meal, knowing that hunger is a signal that I'm burning calories. I'm not afraid of hunger pangs. I can always have a healthy snack of fruit or vegetables.
- When my emotions lead to thoughts about eating, I listen to them and nurture their underlying needs. Offering myself acceptance and compassion fully satisfies my emotional hunger and sticks to my ribs better than any junk food.

To increase the frequency of your physical activity, you might prepare statements such as these:

- I choose to take my body for a walk every day. I protect my body from its addiction to sweets and comfort.
- I can watch television when I'm ninety years old. Now I'm choosing to be active and develop a strong, healthy body.
- I'll have plenty of time to watch other athletes play when I'm ninety years old. Now I am the athlete who works out three to six days a week.
- I choose to exercise to build strong muscles that burn fat and because it feels good. Exercise of my leg muscles pumps blood more easily throughout my body, helping my heart muscle to relax.

- Even when I feel tired, I know that getting out of my chair and doing some exercise will bring oxygen to my brain and burn calories that release energy to my body.
- Exercise that takes me out of my office gives me a new view of things and allows my subconscious mind to work on creative solutions.
- This is my body. Certain habits—such as overeating, smoking, and using TV as an escape—are toxic for my body's optimal health. I'm committed to protecting my body from all toxic substances and toxic habits.

After you've challenged distracting thoughts with these statements, you may want to shorten them to more handy examples, such as these used by my clients and myself:

- I've had plenty.
- Please put the rest in a take-out container.
- Hunger is good—it means I'm burning fat.
- I won't starve.
- Fluids are food.
- I savor my food—I don't gobble.
- I only need two spoonfuls of dessert, the first and the last. Those are the only ones I really taste and savor.
- I can always eat celery or apples.
- I can have whatever I want, when I fully choose it.
- My body likes to move, to dance, to work out.
- Watching other people being active and creative reminds me to express my own talents and exercise my own abilities.
- Exercise oxygenates my lungs and my brain.
- Exercise raises my metabolism for twelve hours.
- I enjoy feeling solidly centered in my mind and body.

In keeping with the principles of the Awaken Your Strongest Self program, the ultimate challenge to distracting thoughts and cravings from some archaic fearful part of you is "That's not like me," which means:

- That's my old identity speaking—my limited ego, seeing things from its separated, lonely perspective and coping with its limited resources.
- I now live my life from the perspective of my integrated, Strongest Self.
- I'm no longer the fearful, worried child I once was. Now I'm the adult who has a fearful, worried child to protect and guide.

Angela calls these phrases her "therapy against depression." She's used them to get herself through the first six months of her journey to her goals and to help her lose thirty-six pounds, maintain her commitment to exercise at the gym three times a week, and stop binging except for five occasions. These measurable results encourage me to believe that Angela will reach all her goals within the next six months. But it's the immeasurable, positive changes in her mood and attitude that make both of us certain that she has already succeeded in becoming her wiser, Strongest Self.

Her use of coping plans and statements improved her sense of self-efficacy—the confidence that she could start to work on her goals and have the ability to follow through on them, even when obstacles arose. This is a solid form of confidence based on using more of your brain-cell power—conscious and subconscious—to confront overwhelming tasks and goals and complete them.

True Confidence That You'll Succeed

True confidence is not about winning or losing but is about knowing that regardless of what happens, you'll be at peace with yourself. It doesn't mean you're confident that everything will go along perfectly and that you won't have a setback. Rather, it means that regardless of how things turn out, you're not going to let a setback ruin your life or even your weekend. A major purpose of this whole book is to give you the skills and perspective that enable you to say to yourself, "Regardless of what happens, I'm on your side. I won't make you feel bad. I'm your safety net. Your worth is safe with me."

True confidence means that you'll not allow anyone to judge your worth as a person. It means that whatever happens—or whatever anyone says—you know ahead of time that you'll not abandon yourself, that you'll find a way to lessen self-criticism and pain and maximize happiness and pleasure in your life. True confidence is based on *knowing* that if you fail at achieving your goal, some strong and creative part of you will find a way to persist, pick up the pieces, recover rapidly from disappointment, and get back on track with your mission. (See Appendix D for a list of self-statements that communicate unconditional acceptance.)

15

You *Are* Your Strongest Self

No, no, no . . . meditation hasn't led me to a state of unending peace.
I still get caught. But I stay caught less—not because I'm such a bril-
liant person, but because I'm aware sooner of the pain of caught-ness
and I just won't do it.

—Sylvia Boorstein, *Pay Attention, for Goodness' Sake*

WHEN WE STARTED on this journey a few weeks ago, you may
have been stuck in a rut. You may have wanted to unlock more
of your potential and improve your efficiency and creativity. Or
you simply may have wanted strategies for living more fully and
easily. Some of you may have had moderate to serious problems
with procrastination, workaholism, anxiety, feeling overwhelmed,
or health and fitness issues. Regardless of your reasons, you were
interested enough in changing your situation that you made it to
this last chapter. Some part of you wanted more out of life—
wanted a change and was eager to awaken your Strongest Self
and ignite the power of your higher brain to find it.

As you continue to use the concepts and practices of this
book's four-step program on a daily basis, you'll more consistently occupy the perspective and roles of your Strongest Self,
and you'll recognize more quickly when you're pulled off track
by obsolete patterns. You may at times still get caught in fear,

self-doubt, and ineffective methods of coping. But you'll stay caught less because your sense of self has expanded to include your deeper resources, the integration of lower brain functions, and greater access to the wisdom of your subconscious mind. Why would you put up with the unnecessary pain caused by allowing your ego to struggle separate from its larger support system when connecting to your Strongest Self makes life so much easier, more manageable, creative, and joyful?

Exercising Belief in Yourself

By applying the Awaken Your Strongest Self program to your daily life for the past few weeks, you've built access routes to your executive-brain functions and enabled yourself to shift more easily to the perspective, roles, and voice of your awakened self. The daily use of this program will strengthen neural pathways from your executive-brain to lower brain functions, giving you greater control over former habits and moods. Even in the midst of stressful situations, you'll know that you now have in place healthy alternatives to replace your former patterns. The more you access your deeper resources and wisdom, the more you'll feel their support and presence working for you. Your actions will become increasingly more congruent with your vision of who you wish to be.

You'll be able to regulate your lower brain functions and integrate those parts that once would have kept you stuck in anxiety and worry for days or weeks. Now you've connected them to the compassionate and guiding voice of your Strongest Self. When you're living from your Strongest Self, no single event or person can ruin your life, your weekend, or your evening. Your enhanced ability to deflect distractions, self-criticism, and self-doubt will bring you back on track within seconds, making you optimally effective and productive with minimal downtime.

After you've used the four steps of this book for a few months, practiced the exercises, and experienced a major shift in perspective, continue to explore these questions:

- If you weren't stuck in a limited ego identity, the one you've been conditioned to believe is you, what would you do? Would you take a course in a field or interest that you've only dreamed about? Would you risk taking time off from your job? Would you invest ten hours this week in a project that you've been avoiding?
- If you could expand your identity to include the genius of your subconscious mind, the creativity of the right hemisphere of your brain, and the wisdom of your autonomic nervous system, what dreams would you pursue?
- If you had a guarantee from your Strongest Self that your worth is safe and that even when you *experience* a failure you'll never *be* a failure, what would you try?
- If you knew that whether you lose everything or become outrageously successful you'll always be at peace with yourself, what adventure would you start today?
- If you knew that despite your problems and imperfections your higher self accepts you completely, how calm and peaceful would you feel?

What would you want to tell your children, friends, students, or clients about what they can expect from life? You might want to communicate these ideas to them:

- There's a strong, wise part of you always watching over you. Even when some part of you feels afraid, there's a strong self that has a bigger view of things and more resources than you can imagine.
- External possessions, accomplishments, and other people can't satisfy your deepest needs. It's what's inside you and your relationship with yourself that matters most.

- You need to discover that regardless of what happens, regardless of what anyone says, you can always be safe with your Strongest Self. Then you'll have attained inner peace and truly be successful.

Inner Peace and the Awakened Mind

You began this program by identifying your major problem areas and their symptoms in step 1. You also became aware of negative and self-critical voices that have kept you stuck in destructive patterns. You activated your higher, executive-brain functions by observing, labeling, and identifying your problem areas as originating in small, primitive parts of a much larger, stronger self. This act of observing—as in meditation—lets you know that you have a self that is more than your problems, thoughts, emotions, and impulses. In step 2 you learned how to empower yourself by taking on the roles, perspective, and voice of your Strongest Self. By learning to change your inner dialogue to a more compassionate and understanding voice, you became a more effective self-leader and you identified the parts of you that have been longing to hear from you.

In step 3 you learned how to use the five qualities of your Strongest Self to replace your outdated, destructive patterns with messages that meet your deeper needs. In providing the five qualities of safety, choice, presence, focus, and connection, you took on roles that shifted your perspective and awakened powers you didn't know you had. In step 4 you learned to use your leadership and chairperson roles to integrate all parts of you in a cooperative effort aimed at achieving your higher goals and aligning your actions with your higher values. You added the four stages of effective change to your repertoire of transformative skills. These stages of change ensured that you have the commitment, motivation, and plans to maintain your healthy habits and to remove any problematic patterns.

Through the four steps to unlocking your full potential, you've learned how to connect your conscious mind and ego to right-brain creativity and support. And you've discovered that your lower brain survival functions can cooperate with your higher brain's vision and leadership. Now, it's *you*, as your Strongest Self, who's in a leadership role, capable of creating a meaningful vision, committing to positive change, and determining your higher values and top priorities. It's *you*, as the self, who maintains the perspective that keeps the inner team on track with your values and goals. And it's *you*, as the self, who speaks in a compassionate voice that gains the cooperation of all parts and integrates them into an effective team. As your Strongest Self:

• You no longer limit your identity to your thoughts, feelings, or impulses.
• You no longer waste time trying to make your ego feel confident, motivated, and all-knowing before you choose to take action.
• You no longer spend more than five seconds struggling—beside your self, separated from your larger Strongest Self—before connecting with the new roles, perspective, and voice that empower you to take charge and manage your life.
• You now can say, "I *am* my Strongest Self. I have a new perspective on life and on who I truly am. I'm more than my old habits, fears, or impulses. I now am living from my higher, human brain and my Strongest Self."

In the Introduction, pretests gave you a chance to record your levels of stress, joy, inner peace, and connection as well as your sense of self-efficacy or confidence that you can make positive changes in your life. You can use the posttests in Appendix F to compare where you were when you started reading this book with your current levels and feelings. The comparative scores will show you how much you've progressed and will point out any issues that require more of your attention. If you've skipped over any of the exercises and homework, you owe it to yourself to experience the sense of empowerment gained from shifting to the perspective and roles of your Strongest Self. Your own experience will do so much more for you than I could ever explain with concepts, case examples, or metaphors.

Use this book over and over again as you identify new issues that distract you from the path to living more consistently from your Strongest Self. You'll find that what may have seemed like a major obstacle months ago has become an insignificant, momentary disruption and that you have many more positive ways to respond to life's stressors, challenges, and opportunities. If at any time you hear a voice that says, "But how do I do it?" recognize that question as coming from your separated ego and conscious mind once again trying to struggle alone. Go back to the essential exercise in Chapter 2, connect that part to your larger self, and speak to it from the voice of your Strongest Self.

It's my hope that you've received tremendous benefit from reading this book and that you're on the path to becoming healthier, more effective, centered, self-content, and joyful. Please consider this book and me as members of your larger support system. Here's to you and your awakened Strongest Self!

Journal for Successful Change

AT LEAST TWICE A DAY for two weeks record when you become aware of problematic symptoms. Without trying to change anything—and without criticizing yourself—simply notice and record the thoughts, physical sensations, and emotions that are inconsistent with your higher vision. Notice how you feel and act when you allow your default reactions to go unchallenged for more than a minute or two.

Use the journal on pages 212–213.

Date and Time	Symptom	Physical, Emotional, Verbal Reactions	Behavior/Action, Feelings/Attitude
1.			
2.			
3.			
4.			
5.			
6.			
7.			

8.

9.

10.

11.

12.

13.

14.

Centering Exercise

THIS ONE-MINUTE, twelve-breath exercise transitions your mind from fretting about the past and future to centering in the present—where your body must be. Centering in the present clears your mind of regrets about the past and worries about anticipated problems in the future. As you withdraw your thoughts from these imagined times and problems, you can experience a stress-free vacation in the present. You are practicing a form of centering whenever you engage in moments of the joyful abandon, the easy flow of creativity, or a state of concentration that leads to effortless optimal performance.

Use this exercise each time you start a project. Within just a week or two, your body and mind will learn to naturally let go of tension and focus on working efficiently and optimally in the present.

1. Sit in a chair and begin the exercise by taking three slow breaths, in three parts: (1) inhale, (2) hold your breath and muscle tension, and (3) exhale slowly. With each exhalation:

- Let go of the last telephone call, the difficult commute, and so on. Float down into the chair. Exhale and let go of any unnecessary muscle tension as you feel the support of the chair and the floor.
- Let go of all thoughts and images about work from the past. Clear your mind and your body of all concerns

about what should have or shouldn't have happened in the past. Let go of old burdens.

- Let go of trying to fix your old problems. Take a vacation from trying to fix other people. Let each exhalation become a signal to let go of work and stress from the past.
- Say to yourself, "I release my mind and body from the past."

2. With your next three breaths:

- Let go of all images and thoughts about what you think may happen in the future—all the what ifs.
- Let go of the work of trying to control the future; clear your muscles, your heart, and your mind of all anticipated work and problems, as well as your have tos and to-do lists.
- Say to yourself as you exhale, "I release my mind and body from the future."

3. With your next three breaths:

- Say, "I'm choosing to be in this present moment, in front of this work. There's nothing else to do and nowhere else to be."
- Say, "I notice how little effort it takes to breathe comfortably and to accept just the right level of energy to be in this moment, focused on just this task, now."
- Say, "For the next few minutes, there is nothing much for my conscious mind to worry about. Within this sanctuary my mind and body are safe from the past and the future."
- Say to yourself as you exhale, "I bring my mind into the present, where I am centered within my larger, wiser, Strongest Self."

4. With your next three breaths, count up from one to three: one, becoming more adequately alert with each breath; two, being interested in going rapidly from not knowing to knowing; and three, feeling eager to begin, curious about how much you will accomplish in such a short period of time.

Stress Quiz

THIS IS A QUICK and informal check of life conditions that may be causing you stress.

Assign each question a number from 0 to 5 to indicate its frequency in your life, and then add up the numbers for a total score.

NEVER		SOMETIMES			FREQUENTLY
0	1	2	3	4	5

1. _____ I have a lot on my mind that worries me—at work, at home, or both.
2. _____ I never shut off my beeper or cell phone.
3. _____ My family makes too many demands on me.
4. _____ I don't have enough time for leisure and my personal needs.
5. _____ I feel a great deal of time pressure at work.
6. _____ I feel bad that I've lost or become separated from loved ones in the last two years.
7. _____ I have trouble focusing on a task.
8. _____ I have difficulty communicating with my family, boss, or coworkers.
9. _____ I handle most things alone, with little support from family, friends, or coworkers.
10. _____ I do not have enough say in decisions that affect me.
11. _____ My personal needs are in conflict with my organization or family.

12. _____ People or circumstances keep me from doing what I want to do.

13. _____ I am often fatigued and sleepy.

14. _____ People or things often irritate me.

15. _____ There's considerable illness in my life and that of my family.

16. _____ I have financial concerns and frequently worry about my financial security.

17. _____ My life is one crisis after another.

18. _____ I regularly have headaches (three times a week = 5).

19. _____ I have muscle tension in my shoulders, neck, or back almost every day.

20. _____ I have stomach pains, indigestion, or other digestive problems.

21. _____ I regularly take pain medication, sleeping pills, tranquilizers, etc.

22. _____ I have a tendency to overeat, especially sweets and pastries.

23. _____ I regularly need a drink or two to unwind.

24. _____ I drink more than three cups of coffee or other caffeinated drinks almost every day.

25. _____ I am not satisfied with my sex life.

26. _____ Family, friends, or people at work tell me I drink too much.

27. _____ Most of my time is spent sitting. I get little exercise.

28. _____ I smoke or use tobacco.

29. _____ I have unrealistically high standards for myself.

30. _____ I would like to make changes in my life but don't know how.

_____ **TOTAL**

SCORING

Under 40 You're in great shape!

41–70 Average. You could lower your stress level.

71–90 Near dangerous levels. Start making changes in how you talk to yourself. Begin to take charge of your fight-or-flight response. Reread Chapter 5.

91+ Act now to reduce stress! Change your environment and create internal safety. Identify all dictatorial and critical voices. Find healthy alternatives to your current addictive habits. Reread Chapters 4 and 5. Do the exercises. Practice the self-statements in Appendix D.

Effective Self-Talk

The Voice of Acceptance

WHEN YOU, from the perspective and roles of your Strongest Self, speak the compassionate statements listed on the next page to the frightened and overwhelmed parts of you, you can do the following:

- Create inner peace by connecting your ego to something stronger and wiser than itself.
- Transition to a new, expanded, and robust self-image.
- Gain support and strength to cope with changing situations and relationships.
- Reduce the stress and anxiety of struggling alone, separated from your true self.
- Empower yourself with the protective role, higher perspective, and compassionate voice of your Strongest Self.

This form of inner dialogue is more effective than typical affirmations because *you* are speaking from a higher perspective, role, and voice *to* a smaller part of you—whether you think of that part as childlike, a more primitive brain, your body, or the worrying part of your mind. You have shifted to a perspective and voice that empower you to take on a protective role toward your body and life. Note that you are not asking the frightened, overwhelmed parts of you to be brave, confident, or motivated. You are the one speaking to them from a place of compassion, understanding, and leadership, and you are the one guiding all parts of yourself toward attaining inner peace.

Here are some examples of compassionate self-talk:

- Regardless of what happens in life, you are always worth-while to me.
- Regardless of what you can or cannot do, you are always worthwhile.
- Your worth is not based on what you do but on who you are.
- Regardless of whether you win or lose, you deserve love, pleasure, and freedom from self-criticism.
- Regardless of what happens to you, you deserve to be treated with dignity and respect.
- Regardless of who stays or who goes, I am on your side. I will never abandon you.
- Regardless of how healthy or ill you become, I appreciate the effort, wisdom, and protection given me by you, my body and my spirit.
- Regardless of how negative or intense your emotions become, I acknowledge their validity for you. I am strong enough to be with your emotions.
- Regardless of how uncomfortable others are with you, your feelings, or your body, I will always accept you and remain at peace with you.
- Regardless of what happens in life, I accept you and love you completely.
- Regardless of the health or weakness of your body, you can always heal your spirit.

Effective Habit Change

As PART OF YOUR PLAN to maintain your commitment to your goals and remain resilient to setbacks—Stage IV of effective change—you may find it helpful to practice for two weeks keeping track of your goals, your action steps, when you intend to start, your awareness of possible obstacles or distractions, and the healthy alternatives you'll use to refocus on the path to your goal. After filling in the chart on pages 221–222 for fourteen days, you'll be able to catch your old patterns within a few breaths and replace them with healthy, effective alternatives. Follow the example given on the first line of the chart, adapting it to fit your own goals.

Ultimate Goal	Action	When	Obstacles	Alternatives
"I intend to"	"I will do"	"I will start at"	"I'm tired"	"Yes, and I will choose"
I intend to be trim and strong in six months.	I will go to the gym three times a week.	I will start today at 6:00 P.M.	I'm tired. I'll go tomorrow.	Yes, I'm tired, and I'm choosing to start and will see if I feel better after a few minutes.

1. _____

2. _____

3. _____

4. _____

5. _____

6. _____

7. _____

8. _____

9.

10.

11.

12.

13.

14.

Posttests

Posttest to Measure Your Progress

In the Introduction I encouraged you to record your levels of stress, joy, inner peace, and feelings of connection before starting this process. Now you can use this posttest to measure how much progress you've made and to identify areas where you may need more practice. Imagine that these scales are thermometers to record your current levels of stress, joy, inner peace, and connection. (Note that on the stress scale, a lower score indicates you've made improvement. On the other three scales, a higher score indicates you've made improvement.)

1. Stress
Circle the number that indicates your average level of stress for the past week.

NONE									THE MOST EVER	
0	10	20	30	40	50	60	70	80	90	100

2. Joy
Circle the number that indicates your average level of joy for the past week.

NONE									THE MOST EVER	
0	10	20	30	40	50	60	70	80	90	100

3. Inner Peace

Circle the number that indicates your average level of inner peace for the past week.

NONE										THE MOST EVER
0	10	20	30	40	50	60	70	80	90	100

4. Connection

Circle the number that indicates your average level of feeling connected to something larger than yourself for the past week.

NONE										THE MOST EVER
0	10	20	30	40	50	60	70	80	90	100

Posttest to Measure Changes in Your Intention and Commitment

You can use these five scales to see how much you've awakened your Strongest Self and new brain to put you in charge of your life and to set goals that will be started on, committed to despite obstacles, and achieved. These measures will give you a sense of how much progress you've made and point out areas where you may need more practice.

1. Desire/Motivation

How much do you want to improve, change, and take charge of your life?

DEFINITELY DO NOT										DEFINITELY DO
0	1	2	3	4	5	6	7	8	9	10

2. Ability

To what extent do you see yourself as being capable of making improvements, creating positive change, and taking charge of your life?

INCAPABLE										CAPABLE
0	1	2	3	4	5	6	7	8	9	10

3. Confidence

How confident are you that you will improve, change, and take charge of your life?

NOT VERY CONFIDENT   VERY CONFIDENT

0	1	2	3	4	5	6	7	8	9	10

4. Perceived Control

How much personal control do you feel you now have over making improvements, changing habits, and taking charge of your life?

NO CONTROL   COMPLETE CONTROL

0	1	2	3	4	5	6	7	8	9	10

5. Intention

How often do you intend to use the exercises and concepts in this book to make improvements, change habits, and take charge of your life?

NEVER   FREQUENTLY

0	1	2	3	4	5	6	7	8	9	10

References

Ajzen, I., Brown, T. C., and Carvahal, F. (2004). Explaining the discrepancy between intentions and actions: The case of hypothetical bias in contingent valuation. *Personality and Social Psychology Bulletin*, 30, 1108–1121.

Armitage, C. J., and Conner, M. (2000). Social cognition models and health behaviour: A structured review. *Psychology and Health*, 15, 173–189.

Avero, P., and Calvo, M. G. (2000). Test anxiety and ego-threatening stress: Over- (and under-) estimation of emotional reactivity. *Anxiety, Stress, and Coping*, 13, 143–164.

Bandura, A. (2004). Health promotion by social cognitive means. *Health Education & Behavior*, 31(2), 143–164.

———. (1997). *Self-Efficacy: The Exercise of Control*. New York: W. H. Freeman.

Banyas, C. A. (1999). Evolution and phylogenetic history of the frontal lobes. In B. L. Miller and J. L. Cummings (Eds.), *The Human Frontal Lobes: Functions and Disorders* (pp. 83–106). New York: Guilford Press.

Baum, K., and Trubo, R. (1999). *The Mental Edge: Maximize Your Sports Potential with the Mind/Body Connection*. New York: Perigee.

Biddle, S. J. H. (1999). Motivation and perceptions of control: Tracing its development and plotting its future in exercise and sport psychology. *Journal of Sport & Exercise Psychology*, 21, 1–23.

Bogen, J. E., and Bogen, G. M. (1993). The other side of the brain: The corpus collosum and creativity. *Bulletin of the Los Angeles Neurological Society*, 34, 191–220.

Boorstein, S. (1994). Insight: Some considerations regarding its potential and limitations. *The Journal of Transpersonal Psychology*, 26(2), 95–105.

Borod, J. C. (Ed.). (2000). *The Neuropsychology of Emotion*. New York: Oxford University Press.

Bowlby, J. (1973). *Separation: Anxiety and Anger*. New York: Basic Books.

Bradbury, R. (1990). *Zen in the Art of Writing: Essays on Creativity*. Santa Barbara, CA: Capra Press.

Budd, M. (2000). *You Are What You Say: A Harvard Doctor's Six-Step Proven Program for Transforming Stress Through the Power of Language*. New York: Crown.

Burns, D. (1999). *Feeling Good: The New Mood Therapy*. New York: Avon.

Campbell, J. (1988). *The Power of Myth*. New York: Doubleday.

Carter, R. (1998). *Mapping the Mind*. Berkeley, CA: University of California Press.

Cozolino, L. (2002). *The Neuroscience of Psychotherapy: Building and Rebuilding the Human Brain*. New York: W. W. Norton.

Damasio, A. (2003). *Looking for Spinoza: Joy, Sorrow, and the Feeling Brain*. New York: Harcourt, Inc.

Darley, J. M., and Cooper, J. (Eds.). (1998). *Attribution and Social Interaction: The Legacy of Edward E. Jones*. Washington, DC: American Psychological Association.

Davey, G. C. L., and McDonald, A. S. (2000). Cognitive neutralizing strategies and their use across differing stressor types. *Anxiety, Stress, and Coping*, 13, 115–141.

Davis, B. (1985). *The Magical Child Within You*. Berkeley, CA: Celestial Arts.

Dychtwald, K. (1978). *Body-Mind*. New York: Jove.

Endler, N. S., and Parker, J. D. A. (1990). Multidimensional assessment of coping: A critical evaluation. *Journal of Personality and Social Psychology*, 58, 844–854.

Engler, J. (1986). Therapeutic aims in psychotherapy and meditation. In K. Wilber, J. Engler, and D. Brown (Eds.), *Transformations of Consciousness*. Boston: New Science Library.

Epstein, M. (1988). The deconstruction of the self: Ego and "egolessness" in Buddhist insight meditation. *Journal of Transpersonal Psychology*, 20(1), 61–70.

Erickson, M. H. (1964). An hypnotic technique for resistant patients: The patient, the techniques and its rationale and field experiments. *American Journal of Clinical Hypnosis*, 1, 8–32.

Fadiman, J. (1990). *Unlimit Your Life: Setting & Getting Goals*. Berkeley, CA: Celestial Arts.

Fiore, N. (1989). *The Now Habit: A Strategic Program for Overcoming Procrastination and Enjoying Guilt-Free Play*. New York: Tarcher/Putnam.

———. (1991). *The Road Back to Health: Coping with the Emotional Aspects of Cancer*. Berkeley, CA: Celestial Arts.

Frederick, C., and McNeal, S. (1999). *Inner Strength: Contemporary Psychotherapy and Hypnosis for Ego Strengthening*. Mahwah, NJ: Lawrence Erlebaum.

Frederick, C., and Phillips, M. (1995). Decoding mystifying signals: Translating symbolic communications of elusive ego states. *American Journal of Clinical Hypnosis*, 38(2), 87–96.

Freud, S. (1926/1959). The question of lay analysis. In J. Strachey (Ed. and Trans.), *The Standard Edition of the Complete Psychological Works of Sigmund Freud* (vol. 20, pp. 177–258).

Goldberg, E. (2001). *The Executive Brain: Frontal Lobes and the Civilized Mind*. Oxford: Oxford University Press.

Goldberg, N. (1998). *Writing Down the Bones: Freeing the Writer Within*. Boston: Shambhala.

Gollwitzer, P. M. (1999). Implementation intentions: Strong effects of simple plans. *American Psychologist*, 54, 493–503.

Heimberg, R. G., and Beck, R. E. (2001). *Treatment of Social Fears and Phobias*. New York: Guilford Press.

Helminski, K. E. (1992). *Living Presence: A Sufi Way of Mindfulness & the Essential Self*. New York: Putnam.

Horney, K. (1949). Finding the real self. *American Journal of Psychoanalysis*, 9(3).

Kohut, H. (1977). *The Restoration of the Self.* New York: International Universities Press.

Kouzes, J. M., Posner, B. Z., and Peters, T. (1996). *The Leadership Challenge: How to Keep Getting Extraordinary Things Done in Organizations.* San Francisco: Jossey-Bass.

Lazarus, R., and Folkman, S. (1984). *Stress, Appraisal and Coping.* New York: McGraw-Hill.

Le Doux, J. (1996). *The Emotional Brain.* New York: Simon & Schuster.

Lewis, T., Amini, F., and Lannon, R. (2000). *A General Theory of Love.* New York: Vintage.

Liggett, D. R. (2000). Enhancing imagery through hypnosis: A performance aid for athletes. *American Journal of Clinical Hypnosis*, 43(2), 149–157.

Lippke, S., Ziegelmann, J. P., and Schwarzer, R. (2004). Initiation and maintenance of physical exercise: Stage-specific effects of a planning intervention. *Research in Sports Medicine*, 12, 221–240.

———. (2005). Stage-specific adoption and maintenance of physical activity: Testing a three-stage model. *Psychology of Sport & Exercise*, 6, 585–603.

Loehr, J. E. (1994). *The New Toughness Training for Sports: Mental, Emotional, and Physical Conditioning.* New York: Plume.

Loehr, J. E., and Schwartz, T. (2003). *The Power of Full Engagement: Managing Energy, Not Time, Is the Key to High Performance and Personal Renewal.* New York: Free Press.

Louganis, B. (1995). *Breaking the Surface.* New York: Random House.

MacLean, P. D. (1990). *The Triune Brain in Evolution: Role in Paleocerebral Functions.* New York: Plenum.

Martin, K. A., and Hall, C. R. (1995). Using imagery to enhance intrinsic motivation. *Journal of Sport & Exercise Psychology*, 17, 59–67.

Masterson, J. F. (1988). *The Search for the Real Self: Unmasking the Personality Disorders of Our Age.* New York: Free Press.

Michie, S., and Abraham, C. (2004). Interventions to change health behaviours: Evidence-based or evidence-inspired? *Psychology and Health*, 19(1), 29–49.

Millman, D. (1999). *Body Mind Mastery: Creating Success in Sport and Life.* New York: New Library.

Milne S., Orbell S., and Sheeran P. (2002). Combining motivational and volitional interventions to promote exercise participation: Protection motivation theory and implementation intentions. *British Journal of Health Psychology*, 7, 163–184.

Muller, W. (1993). *Legacy of the Heart: The Spiritual Advantages of a Painful Childhood.* New York: Fireside.

O'Hanlon, B., and Beadle, S. (1999). *Guide to Possibility Land.* New York: W. W. Norton.

Onestak, D. M. (1991). The effects of progressive relaxation, mental practice, and hypnosis on athletic performance: A review. *Journal of Sport Behavior*, 14(4), 247–282.

Ornstein, R. (1986). *Multimind: A New Way of Looking at Human Behavior.* Boston: Houghton Mifflin.

Pally, R. (2000). *The Mind-Brain Relationship (International Journal of Psychoanalysis Key Paper Series).* New York: Other Press.

Palmer, W. (2002). *The Practice of Freedom: Aikido Practices as a Spiritual Guide.* Berkeley, CA: Rodmell.

Pennebaker, J. W. (1997). *Opening Up: The Healing Power of Expressing Emotions.* New York: Guilford Publications.

Phillips, M., and Frederick, C. (1995). *Healing the Divided Self: Clinical and Ericksonian Hypnotherapy for Post-traumatic and Dissociative Conditions.* New York: W. W. Norton.

Prestwich, A., Lawton, R., and Conner, M. (2003). The use of implementation intentions and the decision balance sheet in promoting exercise behaviour. *Psychology and Health*, 18, 707–721.

Preuss, T. M. (1995). Do rats have prefrontal cortex? The Rose-Woolsey-Akert program reconsidered. *Journal of Cognitive Neuroscience*, 7, 1–24.

Raft, D., and Andresen, J. (1986). Transformations in self-understanding after near-death experiences. *Contemporary Psychoanalysis*, 22, 319–346.

Robinson, J. C. (2000). *Ordinary Enlightenment: Experiencing God's Presence in Everyday Life*. Unity Village, MO: Unity House.

Sarason, I. G., Sarason, B. S., and Pierce, G. R. (1990). Anxiety, cognitive interference, and performance: Communication, cognition and anxiety. *Journal of Social Behavior and Personality*, 5, 1–18.

Schwarzer, R. (2001). Social-cognitive factors in changing health-related behaviors. *Current Directions in Psychological Science*, 10(2), 47–51.

———. (1992). Self-efficacy in the adoption and maintenance of health behaviours: Theoretical approaches and a new model. In R. Schwarzer (Ed.), *Self-Efficacy: Thought Control of Action* (pp. 217–243). Bristol, PA: Taylor & Francis.

———. (1996). Thought control of action: Interfering self-doubts. In I. Sarason, G. Pierce, and B. Sarason (Eds.), *Cognitive Interference*. Hillsdale, NJ: Erlbaum.

Schwarzer, R., and Renner, B. (2000). Social-cognitive predictors of health behavior: Action self-efficacy and coping self-efficacy. *Health Psychology*, 19(5), 487–495.

Seligman, M. E. P. (2002). *Authentic Happiness: Using the New Positive Psychology to Realize Your Potential for Lasting Fulfillment*. New York: Free Press.

———. (1990). *Learned Optimism: How to Change Your Mind and Your Life*. New York: Knopf.

Seligman, M. E. P., Steen, T. A., Park, N., and Peterson, C. (2005). Positive psychology progress: Empirical validation of interventions. *American Psychologist*, 60(5), 410–421.

Senecal, C., and Nouwen, A. (2000). Motivation and dietary self-care in adults with diabetes: Are self-efficacy and autonomous self-regulation complementary or competing constructs? *Health Psychology*, 19(5), 452–457.

Showers, C. (1992). Compartmentalization of positive and negative self-knowledge: Keeping bad apples out of the bunch. *Journal of Personality and Social Psychology, 62,* 1036–1049.

Siegel, D. (2001). *The Developing Mind: How Relationships and the Brain Interact to Shape Who We Are.* New York: Guilford Press.

Sperry, R. (1982). Some effects of disconnecting the cerebral hemispheres. *Science,* 217, 1223–1226.

Spielberger, C. D., and Vagg, P. R. (1995). Test anxiety: A transactional process model. In C. D. Spielberger and P. R. Vagg (Eds.), *Test Anxiety: Theory, Assessment, and Treatment* (pp. 3–14). Washington, DC: Taylor & Francis.

Suinn, R. M. (1993). Imagery. In R. Singer, M. Murphy, and L. Tennant (Eds.), *Handbook of Research on Sport Psychology* (pp. 492–510). New York: Macmillan.

Taylor, S. E., and Brown, J. D. (1988). Illusion and well-being: A social psychological perspective on mental health. *Psychological Bulletin,* 103, 193–210.

Temple-Thurston, Leslie. (2000). *The Marriage of Spirit.* Santa Fe, NM: CoreLight Publications.

Waldroop, J., and Butler, T. (2000). *Maximum Success: Changing the 12 Behavior Patterns That Keep You from Getting Ahead.* New York: Doubleday.

Watkins, J. G., and Watkins, H. (1997). *Ego States: Theory and Therapy.* New York: W. W. Norton.

Watt, D. F. (1990). Higher cortical functions and the ego: Explorations of the boundary between behavioral neurology, neuropsychology, and psychoanalysis. *Psychoanalytic Psychology,* 7(4), 487–527.

Wheatley, Margaret J. (1992). *Leadership and the New Science: Learning About Organization from an Orderly Universe.* San Francisco: Berrett-Koehler Publishers, Inc.

Index